M000107571

The Hunter's
COOKBOOK

STEVE & ANNIE CHAPMAN

HARVEST HOUSE PUBLISHERS
EUGENE, OREGON

Scripture quotations are taken from the New American Standard Bible®, © 1960, 1962, 1963, 1968, 1971, 1972, 1973, 1975, 1977, 1995 by The Lockman Foundation. Used by permission. (www.Lockman.org)

Lyrics and poems © Steve Chapman, Times & Seasons Music, Inc., BMI. All rights reserved.

Some stories are adapted from Steve Chapman, *A Look at Life from a Deer Stand,* gift book ed. (Eugene, OR: Harvest House Publishers, 2005), used by permission; Steve Chapman, *A Hunter Sets His Sights* (Eugene, OR: Harvest House Publishers, 2005), used by permission; and Annie Chapman and Heidi Chapman Beall, *Entertaining Angels* (Eugene, OR: Harvest House Publishers, 2009), used by permission.

Backcover authors' photo © 2012 by Nathan Chapman

Cover photo © iStockphoto / Thinkstock

Cover by Koechel Peterson and Associates, Minneapolis, Minnesota

Illustrations by Steve Chapman. Copyright © 2011 Steve Chapman. All rights reserved.

Interior design by Katie Brady Design, Eugene, Oregon

THE HUNTER'S COOKBOOK
Copyright © 2012 by Steve and Annie Chapman
Published by Harvest House Publishers
Eugene, Oregon 97402
www.harvesthousepublishers.com

Library of Congress Cataloging-in-Publication Data

Chapman, Steve.
 Hunter's cookbook / Steve and Annie Chapman.
  pages cm
 ISBN 978-0-7369-4867-8 (pbk.)
 ISBN 978-0-7369-4868-5 (eBook)
1. Cooking (Game) 2. Cookbooks. I. Chapman, Annie. II. Title.
 TX751.C43 2012
 641.6'91—dc23

                                                                    2011048660

All rights reserved. No part of this publication may be reproduced, stored in a retrieval system, or transmitted in any form or by any means—electronic, mechanical, digital, photocopy, recording, or any other—except for brief quotations in printed reviews, without the prior permission of the publisher.

Printed in China

12 13 14 15 16 17 18 19 20 / RDS-KB / 10 9 8 7 6 5 4 3 2 1

Contents

*We want to thank these folks for
their contributions:*

Willie B

Emmitt and Heidi Beall

Chuck and Kathy Bentley

Kenneth and Evelyn Bledsoe

Carey Bratusek

Travis Cadle

Paul J. and Lillian Chapman

Curt and Delight Christman

Karl and Alice Click

Bobby Emfinger

Joe and Ginny Emmert

Christie (Bonecutter) Francis

JJ Hankins

Joel and LaBreeska Hemphill

Don and Doris Hicks

Chuck Loebsack

James Mayo

Randy and Dena Petrich
(www.huntingmontana.com)

George Reidel

Donnie (Boog) Reynolds

Bob Roberts

Kay Dekalb Smith

Donnie Tyndall

Lindsey and Susan Williams
(http://wildlifeinthewoods.blogspot.com/)

And a special thanks to
David R. Quick
(www.handloadingforhunting.com)

Introduction

by Annie Chapman

THE HUNTER'S COOKBOOK was a welcomed writing project for Steve and me. For the past several years Steve has been busy writing books to inspire men with the insights he's gleaned from the outdoors, while I've been occupied with addressing topics that appeal to women. Now, for the first time in a long time, we get to be a writing team.

Steve's eagerness to work on this book was on the tip of his fingers. He's always looking for a reason to pen more stories about hunting and fishing. I chuckle at what he usually says when he heads out the door to enjoy a deer hunt or go to a lake with his rod and reel: "Hey, babe, I'm off to do more book research!"

My enthusiasm for this writing came easy for two reasons. First, it is a pleasure to provide a collection of wild game recipes we've enjoyed through the years. The main dishes favored by our family (and relatives, friends, and friends of friends) include mostly venison, elk, and turkey, so those sections contain more entries. Thankfully, other contributors' palates range wider, so we've included some of their favorite recipes for other species.

The second reason I gladly got involved has much to do with growing up on a farm in West Virginia. Although my childhood included a few more creature comforts than my parents had growing up (a fancier woodstove, more efficient water pump, and eventually indoor plumbing), I still recall a time when self-sufficiency was a necessary way of life. For example, our family lived quite a distance from a well-stocked grocery store, and there certainly were no restaurants close by. Our trips to town were limited to occasional runs for staples, such as flour and sugar. For the most part, the rest of our shopping was done in our garden.

In my younger years, we didn't have a refrigerator or freezer, so we canned and cured our vegetables and meats...or ate them before they spoiled. Except in the winter when there may have been a spare hog or steer to butcher and the occasional barnyard chicken to chase down and prepare, much of the animal protein our family enjoyed came from the woods, fields, and streams of the farmland around us via the hunting and fishing skills of my dad and, later, my brothers.

From deer to grouse, from squirrels to catfish, the range of consumable critters was intensely valued. Without the harvest of the land, we wouldn't have been as nourished as we were, especially during the leaner economic times.

Because of my deep appreciation for the natural resources God provides that helped sustain my parents, my five siblings, and me, I'm excited about offering a book that will help you appreciate and utilize the bounty of the land. I sincerely hope you will find this book a useful resource for savoring the rewards of the hunt. The hunting and fishing stories Steve has included, which I suggest you read aloud during dinner, give an added dimension to this cookbook that is unique and entertaining. May all the information be used to bless those who put their feet under your table.

Annie Chapman

Annie and Steve Chapman

Part 1
BIG GAME

VENISON

IN THE EARLY 1900s, THE WHITE-TAILED DEER POPULATION was thought to be as low as 500,000 in North America. Thankfully conservation and good hunting regulations have helped increase and sustain the population at healthy levels. Estimates today have the overall herd at more than 20 million, plenty of deer to do their part in nature's life cycle, to let us enjoy watching them, and to allow us to safely harvest some for our tables. Along with the joy of the fair chase, I thoroughly enjoy the other benefit hunting brings, as evidenced in this little poem I wrote several years ago.

THE RECIPE

I saw the deer and took its life
Then gave it to my skillful wife
She added leeks and tall morels
A secret spice I dare not tell
And deep-red fruit of tomato vines
Legumes and fire and evening time
Bread of wheat and coffee hot...
She made me glad I took the shot!

What a wonderful food source God has given us in the deer! One of the advantages of using venison is the lack of fat content. If you're interested in keeping your diet healthy and nutritious, then deer meat is a viable alternative. A good hunting buddy of Steve's had heart bypass surgery. He said he feared that the nutritionist in charge of tweaking his diet would eliminate his favorite meat. Much to his delight, she said he could eat all the venison he wanted. It's considered heart friendly.

So whether whitetail, mule deer, coastal black-tail, or any of the imported exotics, we can be grateful for the sustenance they provide. And there might be as many ways to prepare deer for consumption as there are deer to consume! The following recipes have been enjoyed by many over the years. We hope you enjoy them too.

Venison Cooking Tips

- An important key to a good venison meal is to make sure the raw meat is prepared correctly. Clean away all fat, silver skin (the white membrane), tendons, and connective tissue. Remove the bones. Never cut into the bone when deboning or preparing venison. Cut around the bone to remove the meat. Put the carefully cleaned meat in a large bowl of cold water with a generous amount of salt. Cover and place in the refrigerator. Let the meat sit for a few hours (even a day), and then drain. Rinse the salt off. Now it's ready to freeze or cook.

- Never freeze wild big game in plastic wrap. Several layers of freezer paper will help to avoid freezer burn, which venison is especially susceptible to because of its low fat, high water content. Be sure to date the freezer packages and use meat within eight months.

- To avoid any gamy taste, let the meat thaw slowly in the refrigerator. This may take a couple of days. Never use hot water to hurry the thawing process. If you need to quickly thaw the meat, leave the venison in the freezer paper and let it sit in cold water.

- There are two basic cuts of meat to be used in preparing venison. The more tender cuts of meat come from muscles that are not used a lot, including the back (the coveted back tenderloin called backstrap) and parts of the legs. These cuts should not be overcooked and can be prepared rather quickly. The cuts that come from the deer's "working" muscles that are used vigorously in the everyday life of the animal should be cooked at a lower temperature and for a longer period of time for best results. A Crock-Pot is ideal.

- Because of its lack of grease, venison tends to dry out. One remedy is to use a moist cooking method, such as stewing, braising, or boiling. When cooking meat that tends to be less tender, be sure to cook it longer and more slowly. A Crock-Pot is a perfect solution when preparing these cuts of meat. Add a packet of dry soup mix with some water and onions, and you will not be disappointed.

- If you use a dry-cooking method (grilling or broiling), be sure to reduce the cooking time. Cook the meat less well done than you might otherwise, and baste the meat while it cooks so it won't dry out.

- Venison should be served immediately after grilling. If you let the meat cool, the fiber in the muscles will firm up and the meat will be less tender.

- How can you be sure wild game meat is done? Use the "fork tender" method. If you can cut it easily with a fork, it's done.

- When frying with butter, make sure the heat isn't hot enough to burn the butter.

- When frying with oil, remember that really hot oil causes the meat to tighten and become less tender.

Venison Stroganoff Delight

1 lb. ground venison
1 medium onion, thinly sliced
8 oz. mushrooms, fresh, cleaned, and stemmed
1 clove garlic, fresh, minced
2 T. olive oil
1 T. Worcestershire sauce

1 12-oz. pkg. egg noodles
1 10.5-oz. can cream of mushroom soup
1 10.5-oz. can beef broth
½ cup sour cream
1 pkg. beef and mushroom dry soup mix

Cook ground venison and drain in colander, removing as much fat as possible. (If desired, you can rinse it under warm water to remove more fat.) Place meat in a 6-quart pan and set aside.

In a skillet, sauté onions, mushrooms, and garlic in olive oil. Add Worcestershire sauce and simmer.

Prepare egg noodles according to package instructions. Drain and set aside.

Whisk soup, broth, dry soup mix, and sour cream in a bowl. Stir mixture into meat and bring to boil. Immediately reduce heat and simmer uncovered for a few minutes.

Serve hot over the egg noodles.

Tip: With the meat and starch taken care of, add a green salad and supper is ready!

Venison Burger Casserole

1 lb. ground venison
8-oz. pkg. egg noodles
1 cup celery, chopped
1 cup onion, chopped
3 cloves garlic, minced
1 cup green bell pepper, diced

4 T. butter
1 15-oz. can tomato sauce
1 tsp. salt
¼ tsp. black pepper
1 cup cheddar cheese, shredded

Cook and drain the venison burger.

Prepare egg noodles according to package instructions. Drain and set aside.

Sauté celery, onion, garlic, and bell pepper in butter. Add tomato sauce, salt, and pepper and stir. Add egg noodles to mixture and stir.

Bake at 350° for 30 to 40 minutes. Make sure it is nice and bubbly all over.

Cover meat mixture with cheese and put back into the oven until the cheese is melted.

Tip: This casserole usually feeds six.

Stir-fry Venison

1 lb. venison backstrap or steak
nonstick cooking spray
1 T. olive oil
1 large onion, chopped
1 bell pepper, thinly sliced
3 cloves garlic, minced

1 T. Worcestershire sauce
   (gluten free optional)
1 tsp. hot sauce
1 tsp. cornstarch
¼ cup water
2 cups rice, cooked

Cut venison into strips. (Venison is easier to cut if partially frozen.)

Coat a wok with cooking spray or use a heavy, lightly greased skillet. Add oil and heat on medium high until hot. Add venison and stir-fry 1 minute. Add vegetables and stir-fry until veggies reach desired tenderness. Now add sauces and mix well.

In a separate bowl, mix the cornstarch and water. Add to meat and vegetables, stirring constantly until mixture thickens.

Serve over rice.

Tip: This recipe usually feeds four people.

Best Ever Venison Roast

3 lbs. venison roast	3 T. oil
salt	1 large onion
pepper	1 28-oz. can crushed tomatoes
garlic powder	1 cup water
1 cup flour	hot sauce to taste

Trim the roast of visible fat. Score the roast with thin cuts on the diagonal to help the meat be more tender. Sprinkle all sides of meat with salt, pepper, and garlic powder. Dredge in flour.

Pour oil in frying pan and heat until hot. Carefully place roast in oil and brown on all sides.

Remove meat from frying pan and place in roaster or covered pan.

Put the remaining ingredients on the meat and place in oven.

Bake at 300° for three hours or until done.

Serves 10 to 12 people.

Tip: Use the drippings to make Poor Man's Gravy (page 241).

Venison Meatballs

2 lbs. ground venison	1½ cups water
nonstick cooking oil	¼ tsp. garlic powder
1 envelope onion soup mix	1 tsp. oregano
1 cup ketchup	1 T. Worcestershire sauce

Form ground venison into meatballs. Brown them in a lightly greased skillet. Remove from stove.

Mix remaining ingredients together. Pour sauce over meatballs and put into oven.

Bake at 350° for 1 hour or until done.

Tip: Serve with spaghetti and toasted Italian bread.

Venison Meatballs Supreme

½ lb. ground venison	1 tsp. parsley
1 lb. ground round hamburger	1 egg
1 can water chestnuts, diced	1½ tsp. salt
¾ cup bread crumbs, dry and fine	⅛ tsp. pepper
1 tsp. Worcestershire sauce	½ cup milk

Sauce

1 13.5-oz. bottle ketchup	1 10.5-oz. jar currant jelly

Meatballs

Mix together all ingredients, and roll into walnut-sized balls.

Bake on ungreased cookie sheet at 350° for 40 minutes.

Sauce

In a pan, heat jelly and ketchup together and bring to a boil.

Pour over meatballs and heat again, simmering until the meatballs and sauce are bubbly and all the flavors have mingled.

Serve hot or at room temperature. A great party food served with tooth-picks.

Tip: Venison tastes best when it is served in a combination of sweet and salty flavors. The currant jelly gives this dish the sweetness that will make it more palatable to those who are not venison fans...yet.

SOUL FOOD

Commit your way to the LORD, trust also in Him, and He will do it. He will bring forth your righteousness as the light and your judgment as the noonday (Psalm 37:5-6).

Venison Loaf

2 pkgs. crescent rolls
1 lb. ground venison
1 lb. ground pork or turkey sausage
1 medium onion, chopped
1 24-oz. jar spaghetti sauce
1 16-oz. container of
   small-curd cottage cheese

1 egg
½ cup Parmesan cheese
16 oz. mozzarella cheese
½ cup milk
¼ cup sesame seeds

In a 9 x 13 pan, stretch out one package of crescent rolls, forming a solid rectangle of dough.

Brown the ground venison, sausage, and onion. Drain off fat. Add spaghetti sauce and stir.

In another bowl, mix cottage cheese, egg, and Parmesan cheese.

Now in the pan, layer the ingredients as follows:

½ of meat mixture
cottage cheese mixture
½ of mozzarella cheese

rest of meat mixture
rest of mozzarella cheese

Unfold the second package of crescent rolls and stretch out to form one rectangle. Lay it on top of the meat and cheese mixture. Seal the edges of dough together. Brush a little milk on top of crust and sprinkle on sesame seeds.

Bake at 350° for 45 minutes. Let cool 15 minutes before serving.

Tip: Serve with Evelyn's Potato Salad (page 216)

Easy Venison Meat Loaf

1 lb. ground venison
1 lb. hamburger
2 eggs

¼ cup ketchup
½ tsp. seasoned salt
1 tsp. curry powder

Mix together all ingredients and form into a loaf.

Bake at 375° for 30 minutes or until done.

Tip: This tasty and easy main dish is great for teaching young children or grandchildren to cook. Watch their faces as they announce to the family that they made supper!

Easy and Hearty Venison Sausage Chowder

1 lb. ground venison sausage   1 15-oz. can potato soup
1 15-oz. can cream-style corn

Brown sausage in a skillet, drain, and put into a Crock-Pot. Pour the creamed corn and potato soup into the Crock-Pot and stir.

Turn Crock-Pot to low setting and cook for 6 to 8 hours or turn to high for shorter cooking time of 3 to 4 hours.

Old Timer Mountaineer Hash

1 medium onion, chopped   1 tsp. chili powder
1 medium green pepper, chopped   ¼ tsp. pepper
3 T. butter   ½ cup rice, uncooked
1 lb. ground venison   1 tsp. salt
2 cups canned tomatoes, undrained
   and chopped

Cook onion and pepper in butter until the onion is yellow. Add ground venison and cook until mixture falls apart. Drain fat.

Add tomatoes, chili powder, pepper, rice, and salt. Mix and pour into greased baking dish. Cover.

Bake at 350° for 45 minutes.

SOUL FOOD

How sweet are Your words to my taste! Yes, sweeter than honey to my mouth! From your precepts I get understanding; therefore I hate every false way (Psalm 119:103-04).

Venison and Beef Meat Loaf

1 medium onion, diced	1 egg
1 or 2 garlic cloves, crushed	1 pkg. onion soup mix
½ lb. bacon, chopped	½ cup oatmeal, dry
1 lb. ground venison	salt
1 lb. ground hamburger	pepper

Topping

1 cup ketchup	2 T. mustard (or honey mustard)
2 T. Worcestershire sauce	

Sauté onion, garlic, and bacon in a skillet. (The bacon doesn't have to fully cook because it will be baked.) Drain grease, remove from skillet, and allow mixture to cool.

Place ground venison and ground beef in a large bowl. Add egg, onion soup mix, and dry oatmeal. Add onion, garlic, bacon mixture and mix. Put into loaf pan. Salt and pepper the top.

Topping

Combine ketchup, Worcestershire sauce, mustard. Spread on top of meat loaf.

Bake at 375° for 45 minutes.

Favorite Venison Meat Loaf

2 eggs	¼ cup green peppers, chopped
1½ lbs. ground venison	1 tsp. salt
1 8-oz. can tomato sauce	1 tsp. pepper
½ cup bread crumbs	dash dried thyme
½ cup onion, chopped	dash dried marjoram

Beat two eggs together. Add remaining ingredients, mixing well. Put in loaf pan.

Bake at 350° for 1 hour 15 minutes.

The High Cost of Free Meat

CHUCK AND KATHY BENTLEY AND THEIR CHILDREN moved into the house across the field from us in the late 1990s. During our first conversation as new neighbors, Chuck and I (Steve) discovered we did similar work—we were musicians. Chuck had just finished recording a CD, and he gave us a copy. The production was wonderful. Because our very talented son had gone to college leaving us without an in-house producer, we asked Chuck for his producer's name and contact information. The name he gave us was Lindsey Williams.

Proving that it really can be a small world, nearly a decade earlier Lindsey had given our son, Nathan, guitar lessons. Knowing Lindsey's production and instrumental skills, as well as his cordial demeanor, we connected with him and promptly got started recording a new CD. During the recording of "This House Still Stands," Lindsey and I discovered our mutual interest in hunting. We managed to not let our talk about guns and chasing critters interfere with recording music, but it wasn't easy.

As they say, "the rest is hysterical." It was comical how quickly we bonded over hunting. We couldn't wait for deer season to start! Finally opening day arrived. I was especially excited about including Lindsey in my hunting plans because I'd found out he'd not yet bagged a whitetail. There's hardly anything that gives a veteran hunter more satisfaction than helping a first-timer experience the thrill of success. When it finally happened, I'm not sure which of us felt more elation.

While we've since had many great moments of triumph in the woods together, including the downing of "Doezilla" (Lindsey's eye-popping 150-pound Tennessee doe) and our unforgettable "double doe" morning, his first deer remains one of our all-time favorite memories. But we're not the only ones who took special note of Lindsey's first deer. His wife, Susan, noticed it too. In fact, there were details of her hubby's exploit that probably would have gone unmentioned had she not documented them in her blog. With her permission, we share her well-written "account" of Lindsey's hunt.

There's One Born Every Minute

by Susan Williams

No, I am not referring to a spike in the deer population. I reference, of course, that famous quote by P.T. Barnum, the great American showman, businessman, and scam artist, he of the Ringling Brothers, Barnum and Bailey Circus fame. Barnum is the oft-quoted source of the famous phrase: "There's a sucker born every minute."

But since you're reading this blog, I am going to take a wild guess and speculate that I might not be the only sucker in these here parts. There might be a few more of you out there who, just as I did, bought into the "Big Lie."

To what big lie do I refer, you ask? This sucker, er, innocent, bought into the idea her husband cleverly used to sell her on hunting. Not that he would *purposefully* try to manipulate me, but here's how it went down.

One day I was in the kitchen, minding my own business, cooking something that was doubtless both delicious and economical for dinner because, after all, I'm a pretty good cook. But even more importantly, I know we aren't made out of money, so part of my job as chief cook and bottle washer is to watch for sales at the grocery store and keep our food costs down.

Meat is so expensive. In fact, we hardly ever ate red meat due to the expense and my frugality and desire to live within our hard-earned means (she said as she polished up her halo and batted her eyelashes virtuously).

So one day my sweet husband, Lindsey, cozies up to me in the kitchen.

Him: "Mmm. That smells good. Whatcha makin'?"

Me: "Oh…just a roast chicken."

Him: "Mmm. That'll be great. Hey, hon, you know…I've been thinking…"

Me: "Mm hmm…" I was concentrating on sprinkling spices on the delicious (and cheap!) chicken.

Him: "You know, Steve mentioned the other day that he'd be happy to take me hunting with him. And it occurred to me that hunting might be a really good hobby for me to take up. Because, after all, there's *free meat!*"

Me: "Hmm…" So I'm standing there thinking, "Free meat? Free meat sounds good. And our friend Steve is an expert hunter. He could really teach my man how to be a successful hunter. And then we'd have all that *free meat.* Think of the *savings* on our food bills through the year."

Me: "Well, okay, I guess. That might be good."

Yup. That's about how it went down. And let me tell you, if there really is one born every minute, that was my minute. Because here's how all that *free meat* happened that year:

Hunting license: $135
Gun: $175
Ammo: $50
Camo clothes: $50
Boots: $80

And these are very conservative estimates! And lest we forget, where were we going to store all that *free meat*? We purchased a freezer: $500 (honestly, I'm grateful for it, but still…).

And then there were the "processing fees" once the *free meat* had been procured: $75.

That first year alone, my husband shot a $1000 deer. And I thought I was the trophy wife. Harrumph! And now each year there are guns, gadgets, and gewgaws that must be added to supplement the arsenal:

Bow: $400 to $800
Arrows: $55
Other guns: $350
Rain gear: $65
Blind: $400
Special shower soap: $5.50
Special laundry soap: $6.75
Animal calls: $40 to $50
Decoys of various species: $ (who even knows?)

In the interest of being charitable, I am not even going to mention that little trip across the continent to hunt elk in Colorado.

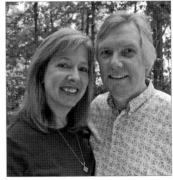

Now you might think I'm ungrateful for all the wonderful, delicious game we eat each year. And if you think that, you'd be wrong. I have learned how to cook it, and cook it deliciously. I'm grateful for the health benefits that come from eating meat that is truly free range and low in fat. I'm grateful for the joy it brings my husband when he comes home from a day in the woods enjoying God's beautiful creation.

Susan and Lindsey Williams

I'm grateful for the camaraderie he shares with Steve, who has become not only a mentor but a true brother.

I'm thankful that their friendship has bonded our family closer to Annie, and to their wonderful children, and grandchildren. Blessing after blessing has come into our lives because I encouraged my dear husband that day to follow his bliss, to pursue a hobby that brings him joy and satisfaction. If I were asked the question all over again, I'd respond the same way. It's been totally worth it. But *free meat*? Not so much!

SOUL FOOD

Shout joyfully to God, all the earth...Say to God, "How awesome are Your works!"...Come and see the works of God, who is awesome in His deeds toward the sons of men (Psalm 66:1,3,5).

Susan's Venison Meatballs

3 cups day-old Italian bread, cut into
   1-inch cubes
2 lbs. ground venison
3 eggs, beaten
3 garlic cloves, minced
¾ cup Pecorino Romano cheese,
   grated (or Parmesan cheese,
   grated)
¼ cup Italian flat-leaf parsley, finely
   chopped

¼ cup pine nuts, toasted
½ tsp. + 1 tsp. salt (coarse-grain
   sea salt preferred)
½ tsp. black pepper, freshly ground
1 lb. spaghetti
1½ cups tomato sauce
½ cup Parmigiano Reggiano
   (Parmesan cheese), grated

Preheat the oven to 375°.

Toast the pine nuts by sautéing them for two minutes until lightly brown.

In a shallow bowl, soak the bread cubes in a cup of water for a minute or two. (Use the best quality bread possible so it has a little oomph and won't turn to mush.) Drain the bread cubes and squeeze with your fingers to press out excess moisture.

In a large bowl, combine the bread cubes, venison, eggs, garlic, Pecorino Romano, parsley, pine nuts, ½ teaspoon salt, and pepper. Mix with your hands.

With wet hands, form meatballs the size of golf balls. (If desired, you can use an ice cream scoop to form the meatballs.) Make sure they are uniform in size. Place them on a cookie sheet or in a mini muffin tin.

Bake for 15 to 20 minutes until nicely brown.

Bring 6 quarts of water to boil in a large pot and add 1 teaspoon salt. Add spaghetti, cook according to package instructions, and drain.

In a 10- or 12-inch sauté pan, combine tomato sauce and meatballs. Heat until meatballs are hot all the way through.

Put the pasta into the sauté pan with the meatballs and toss gently to mix.

Divide onto plates and sprinkle with Parmagiano Reggiano.

Venison Sausage Breakfast Burrito

1 lb. venison sausage
1 small onion, chopped
12 eggs
½ cup water
1 can green chilies
8 flour tortillas

nonstick cooking spray
1 cup cheddar cheese
½ cup sour cream
½ cup Quick and Easy Salsa
    (page 208)

Brown venison sausage and onion. Drain fat.

Beat eggs and combine with water. Stir in green chilies. Pour into sausage and onion mixture.

Cook until eggs have no liquid remaining, being careful not to overcook.

Spray a flat skillet with oil and heat tortillas until they turn light brown.

Fill each tortilla with scrambled egg mixture. Top with cheese, sour cream, and Quick and Easy Salsa.

Venison Quesadillas

Marinade

2 T. lime juice or the juice of 2 limes
1 tsp. cumin
1 garlic, crushed

dash of salt
2 T. Worcestershire sauce

Quesadillas

venison, thinly sliced and marinated
2 T. olive oil
onions
green, red, and yellow peppers

flour tortillas, large
cheddar or other cheese, shredded
butter

Optional: cilantro, tomatoes, black beans, corn, other vegetables

Optional toppings: Quick and Easy Salsa (page 208), sour cream, Fruit Chipotle
Chutney (page 219)

Combine marinade ingredients in a ziplock plastic bag. Add thinly sliced
venison and refrigerate for at least 30 minutes. Remove meat from marinade
and sauté in olive oil until done. Set meat aside.

Sauté onions and sliced green, red, and yellow peppers to desired tenderness.
Set aside.

On a flour tortilla, place cheese, meat, and vegetable mixture. Add cilantro,
tomatoes, black beans, corn, and any other vegetables desired. Fold or roll
the tortilla and place on an amply buttered grill or skillet. Heat until the
quesadilla is warm throughout and golden brown on the outside.

Serve with Quick and Easy Salsa, sour cream, or Fruit Chipotle Chutney.

SOUL FOOD
*The LORD is near to the brokenhearted and saves those
who are crushed in spirit* (Psalm 34:18).

Sweet and Salty Crock-Pot Venison

venison roast
salt
pepper
Tony's Cajun Seasoning
1 32-oz. can beef broth
2 beef bouillon cubes mixed with
   2 cups hot water
1 cup cooking wine or sherry
   (wine's acidic quality tenderizes
   meat) or 1 cup beef broth

1 18-oz. jar red currant jelly
1 large red onion, sliced
2 T. cornstarch
2 cups carrots,
   cut on the diagonal
8 oz. mushrooms
4 large potatoes, cubed

Rinse venison roast in cold water and pat dry. Rub with ample amounts of salt, pepper, and Tony's Cajun Seasoning. Set aside.

In a large Crock-Pot, pour beef broth, beef bouillon with water, cooking wine, and red currant jelly. Stir until everything is mixed well. Add venison and onion.

Cook on medium high heat all day.

Two or three hours before serving, mix cornstarch in 4 tablespoons of cold water and whisk, dissolving lumps. Mix into Crock-Pot contents to thicken to a terrific gravy consistency. Add carrots, mushrooms, and potatoes, and continue to cook.

SOUL FOOD

I will bless the LORD at all times; His praise shall continually be in my mouth. My soul will make its boast in the LORD; the humble will hear it and rejoice. O magnify the LORD with me, and let us exalt His name together (Psalm 34:1-3).

Pan-fried Venison

1 cup all-purpose flour	2 T. olive oil
1 tsp. salt	2 T. butter
½ tsp. black pepper	venison, cubed
½ tsp. garlic powder	

Mix flour, salt, black pepper, garlic powder (and other spices as desired) in a ziplock bag.

Place venison, a few cubes at a time, into the plastic bag, dredging them in the flour mixture. Remove and set aside.

Melt olive oil and butter in a skillet. Turn burner to medium heat, and fry venison until the desired doneness. (Fully cooked with a crunchy, golden-brown crust tastes great.)

Tip: Serve with delicious Sweet and Sour Sauce (page 248).

Grilled Venison Tenderloins

Annie's Favorite Marinade (page 243)	venison tenderloins or steaks

Marinate steaks for 12 to 24 hours in a ziplock bag stored in the refrigerator.

Put the steaks on the grate over hot coals. Cook approximately 2 minutes on each side, turning only once.

If you're in the woods, wait until there is no flame left in the campfire. Put the steaks on forked sticks and hang the meat 4 inches or so above the coals. Cook 2 minutes each side, turning as needed until well done. Hickory or apple wood is great for grilling steaks.

SOUL FOOD
Behold, God is my helper; the LORD is the sustainer of my soul
(Psalm 54:4).

Delicious Tenderloin Backstrap

Venison Marinade (page 245)
tenderloin (backstrap)
salt
pepper
garlic powder

Tony's Creole Seasoning
onions, thinly sliced
mushrooms, sliced
steak sauce
bacon strips

Marinate meat in Venison Marinade. Remove meat from marinade, rinse in cold water, and pat dry.

Butterfly the tenderloin backstrap, almost cutting it in half. Salt and pepper the inside of the meat. Add garlic powder and Tony's Creole Seasoning. Now lay a bed of thinly sliced onions and sliced mushrooms on top of the seasonings and meat.

Soak kitchen string in water until thoroughly wet, bring the "halves" of meat together, and tie with string. Sprinkle salt, pepper, and garlic powder on the outside, along with any other seasonings desired.

Cover the meat with your favorite steak sauce and let marinate for a couple of hours.

Wrap the tenderloin in strips of bacon and secure with toothpicks. Place the meat on a hot grill over indirect heat and cook until desired doneness. Enjoy!

Tip: Butterfly a chop by cutting it down the middle, leaving about one inch at the bottom. Fold the chop over on the cutting board, creating a nice thick steak.

Venison Steak and Gravy

submitted by Evelyn Bledsoe

3 T. shortening	salt
8 venison steaks	pepper
1 cup + 4 T. all-purpose flour	3 beef bouillon cubes

Heat the shortening in an electric skillet or a large iron skillet.

Tenderize steaks with a mallet or small saucer by pounding until the meat is pulverized and tendons are broken up.

Dredge the meat in 1 cup of flour and put in skillet. Brown the steaks on both sides. Sprinkle with salt and pepper after turning.

Mix the beef cubes with water per package instructions and pour into skillet. Cook slowly until the steaks are done, 2 to 3 hours. Keep adding water as needed to keep meat from drying out. (The broth should come up about halfway on the meat.)

Put 4 T. of flour in a small jar and add 1 cup of cold water. Shake well to blend. Pour flour mixture into the skillet and stir until blended as gravy. Let the steak and gravy simmer for 15 minutes, stirring often—even whisking with a wire utensil—to eliminate lumps.

Tip: Serve hot with mashed potatoes and green beans—and don't forget the Sylvie Biscuits (page 222).

Venison Hot Dog Crowd Pleaser

submitted by Evelyn Bledsoe

4 cups water
3 28-oz. cans tomato puree (or
    tomato paste, canned tomatoes,
    tomato sauce)
10 lbs. ground venison
10 beef bouillon cubes
1 T. sugar
1 T. red pepper flakes
1 large onion, chopped

2 T. garlic powder
2 T. chili powder
1 T. celery seed
1 T. basil
1 T. oregano
1½ T. cumin
½ T. sage
4 dozen hot dogs
4 dozen hot dog buns

Put water and tomato puree into a heavy, 10-quart kettle.

Brown the ground venison a little bit at a time in an iron skillet. Drain the grease, and use paper towels to soak up any additional grease. As the burger browns, add it to the kettle mixture.

When all the burger is in the kettle, cook over medium heat, stirring well. Add beef cubes, sugar, red pepper flakes, and onion. Cover the kettle and bring to a boil. Lower the heat, add all the spices, and cook slowly for approximately 2 hours or until the meat is tender. Stir often as it cooks. Keep skimming off as much grease as possible. Add more water as needed.

After the mixture has cooked 1½ hours, taste to determine if you want to add more of any spice.

Serve sauce by pouring over cooked hot dogs or hot dogs and buns.

SOUL FOOD

Rejoice in the Lord always; again I will say, rejoice! Let your gentle spirit be known to all men. The Lord is near. Be anxious for nothing, but in everything by prayer and supplication with thanksgiving let your requests be made known to God. And the peace of God, which surpasses all comprehension, will guard your hearts and your minds in Christ Jesus (Philippians 4:4-7).

Sloppy Joes

4 lbs. venison burger
2 large onions, chopped
2 large green bell peppers, chopped

1 40-oz. bottle of ketchup
2 T. chili powder
12 hamburger buns

Mix all ingredients in skillet except buns. Cook and stir 1 hour or until done. Add more ketchup if needed for desired thickness.

Serve on or over hamburger buns.

Tip: Coleslaw (page 208) goes great with Sloppy Joes!

Hearty Sausage and Beans

1 15-oz. can white kidney (cannellini) beans
2 15-oz. cans red kidney beans
1 lb. cooked venison sausage, cut into 1-inch pieces
2 large onions, chopped

2 large sweet red peppers, chopped
1 large green bell pepper, chopped
¼ cup brown sugar, packed
2 T. steak sauce
1 T. cider vinegar
1 tsp. Worcestershire sauce

Rinse all beans, drain, and set aside.

In a large skillet, cook sausage for 2 to 3 minutes. Stir in onions and peppers. Cook and stir until sausage is lightly browned and vegetables are tender. Drain.

In a separate bowl, combine brown sugar, steak sauce, cider vinegar, and Worcestershire sauce. Stir the mixture into the skillet of meat and vegetables. Add the beans. Cook and stir until heated through.

SOUL FOOD

The earth is the LORD's, and all it contains, the world, and those who dwell in it (Psalm 24:1).

Christian's First Deer

related by Christian's dad, Curt Christman

OCTOBER 16 STARTED COOL AND SOMEWHAT CLOUDY in our neck of the New York woods. I sat with Christian for his first hunt while his brother, Corwin, bow-hunted a few hundred yards away. Christian and I were hoping to intercept deer coming off the hayfield to our left.

The morning hunt yielded nothing, so we headed home around 9:30 for a short rest and breakfast. The warm fire in the woodstove begged us to stay, but I knew if we stayed too long we would succumb to the desire to close our eyes, thus only dreaming of downing the *big* one. Christian decided he needed warmer clothes, so we headed out. We stopped for some snacks and fuel for our gas-guzzling pickup and then hurried to the co-op to shop for hunting clothes.

A hefty $148 later (out of Christian's pocket), we were off to our afternoon hunt. We moved from our earlier location, and set up in front of some small cedars. After 45 minutes or so, I was feeling drowsy. I told Christian that since he'd spent much of the morning watching the insides of his eyelids while I kept watch for brown furry things, it was his turn to stand watch. I'd only "doesed" for around 10 minutes when I was awaked by the loud kaboom of a muzzleloader. I estimated the distance at 500 yards away. I jumped up and grabbed my gun. Christian was already at full alert as he looked for fleeing deer.

A few seconds later I saw Christian shoulder his gun. A mature doe came to a halt right in front of our position. As she stood broadside and looked back in the direction from which she'd come, I heard Christian's muzzleloader deliver its load. What happened next is something I've enjoyed remembering since that unforgettable day.

As the smoke cleared, I watched Christian's eyes display the thrill of connecting with a big game animal. But then my heart sank as I saw doubt spread across his face as the doe sped away. Drawing from 27 years of deer hunting experience, I knew the deer had been hit. Her high kick and labored-but-hurried departure was proof enough. But Christian didn't know what I knew. Hoping to relieve him of a little bit of his worry, I forced calmness into my voice and said, "Son, quietly reload. After a few minutes, we'll look for the blood trail to follow."

When we walked over to the place of bullet impact, a mere 31 yards away, I looked for the telltale signs that the deer had been wounded. I didn't find any blood or hair. I could see where the dirt had been dug up as she made her escape, but there was hardly any other sign to be found. We tracked as best we could without the advantage of snow or mud. We stopped a short 50 yards later when all indications of a deer on the run were gone. We had no clue which direction she'd gone.

I cautiously wandered over to the edge of the woods where I suspect she'd headed. I stood there a minute or so looking hard for just one more sign of a fast-moving deer. With nothing visible, I made one of the hardest decisions for a hunter—to stop the search and wait. I instructed Christian that if a wounded animal is allowed to lie down and lick its wounds, the chances of finding it are better. Though it was painful for him, he agreed to wait.

I silently whispered a prayer as we settled down, telling the Lord that for Christian's sake we needed some sign that the fleeing doe was hit. In the next instant I could hardly believe what I saw. As I lay my muzzleloader down in the grass at the edge of the woods, I spotted a small but distinct puddle of clear slime. I touched it with my gloved finger and lifted it to my nose. I detected the sour smell of stomach acid. I told Christian to take courage—that his first trophy was definitely hit. If we did the search right, there was a good chance of retrieving her.

At 4:30 we were ready to make our move. I wanted Christian to circle the patch of woods I was about to enter in case I spooked the deer. That way he might have a chance to intercept it on the other side. However, he wanted to be with me if the deer was found, so I gave in. It paid off to stick together because after walking 50 yards, I saw a patch of white fur. As I carefully studied the sight, I could see the snow-white patch was surrounded by grayish brown fur.

I pointed out the doe to my son, and we vigorously gave each other a celebratory handshake and hug. As we started toward the deer, Christian couldn't keep from running ahead to his downed trophy. It was joy beyond measure to see him lean over the doe and then grin ear to ear. We called Corwin on our radio to give him the news. He left his treestand to join us. We later learned that his premature departure spooked a deer as he descended. Oh well!

Christian did a fine job field dressing the 135-pound doe. I walked ahead of my sons as they worked together to drag the prize to the edge of the field and our rig. Christian called his mom on his cell, so when we got home she met us in the driveway with a big smile and a camera ready for taking photos that will be treasured for years to come.

How glad we all were that we didn't let the sleepy bug bite us when we got back to the warm fire that morning. We learned an important lesson about how determination can yield exciting moments, long-lasting memories, and the main ingredient in one of our favorite venison meals we affectionately call "Venzen Sloppy Joes."

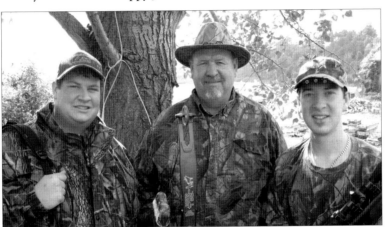

Christian, Curt, and Corwin Christman

Venzen Sloppy Joes

1 lb. ground venison
1 small onion, chopped
1/3 cup red wine or cider vinegar
1/3 cup ketchup
2 T. mustard
1 tsp. salt

1/2 tsp. pepper
1 tsp. garlic powder
1 cup brown sugar (or maple syrup)
4 hamburger buns
1 cup cheddar cheese

Quickly brown the venison and onions. As soon as the red is gone from the meat, add the red wine, ketchup, and mustard. While stirring, add salt, pepper, and garlic powder. Cook for a short time and then slowly stir in the brown sugar. Let cook for at least 15 minutes on low heat.

Layer bread and sloppy joe mixture in a bowl, top with cheddar cheese, and serve.

Tip: Adding tomatoes to meat naturally tenderizes it because the acid in the tomatoes helps break down the fiber of the meat. Tomatoes also help cover any gamy taste.

Venison Steaks

1½ to 2 lbs. venison steaks
1 cup buttermilk

1 cup water

Marinade

2 cloves garlic, minced
3 T. butter, melted
1 tsp. hot sauce
2 T. red wine
2 T. rosemary, freshly chopped
1 sprig thyme, freshly chopped

1 tsp. paprika
1 tsp. dried basil
½ tsp. salt
1 tsp. black pepper
¼ tsp. cayenne pepper
1 T. honey

Steak Preparation

½ cup olive oil

tin foil

The night before, prepare the meat by soaking it in equal parts water and buttermilk. The next morning, pour off the liquid and place the meat in a large bowl or ziplock bag.

Combine the marinade ingredients and pour over the meat. Cover and refrigerate for four hours.

Remove meat from marinade and allow to sit at room temperature for 20 to 30 minutes. Pat steaks dry and coat with olive oil.

Place steaks on a hot grill for 4 to 7 minutes per side. (The time depends on the grill, the thickness of the steaks, and how you prefer them cooked.) When steaks are done, put them on a plate, cover with tin foil, let set for 5 to 10 minutes, and then serve.

Tip: This recipe also works well for a 2-pound venison roast.

The One That Almost Got Away

as told by Curt Christman

I F ANYONE EVER DESERVED TO ACHIEVE the taking of his or her first deer, it was my son Corwin. From the time he could barely pull up his own boots I took him hunting with me. All my children went with me from time to time, often on afternoon hunts but rarely in the early morning hours. Corwin, on the other hand, crawled out of his warm, cozy bed morning after morning. His determination to see me take a deer was stronger than any I've ever seen in a child. At times it seemed almost stronger than my own!

For the previous two years, Corwin had hunted with archery equipment because, in the state of New York, a hunter must be 16 to use a firearm. So Corwin and I toted our bows and arrows many a sleepy morning in hopes of getting close to the elusive whitetail. On this day, as hard as we tried, we were nearing the end of a fruitless season. We had spent many days without seeing any deer, so we were tempted to pack it in. However, our die-hard attitudes prevailed. Once again we crunched our way through the frozen grass and hauled our tired bodies into our deer stands.

After making sure Corwin was safe in his stand and settling my son Christian in his, I went to mine. As I settled in on that Tuesday morning, I sighed deep and offered up a prayer. I rarely pray to take a deer, but desperate times bring desperate measures. I said, "Lord, as much as I would like to get my own deer, I want Corwin and Christian to be successful." We had put a lot of money and hours into the trip, and coming home empty-handed would not be a good thing.

Looking around the cold, damp woods, I resolved to the likelihood that I'd have a long wait. Around 7:15 I heard that telltale sound of large-bodied animals moving through the brush. I spotted movement in the goldenrods about 100 yards out. Two deer were hurrying by, passing in front of me but behind too much brush for a decent shot. The excitement of actually seeing deer kept me content for a while, but boredom and the pressure of going home empty-handed got me thinking of ways to create some action. I called Christian on the cell phone and told him to get ready to put on a drive for Corwin and me. I moved to another fixed stand that a friend had built just off the road overlooking a gas well. Just as I got up on the stand, I spotted Corwin about 250 yards away wildly waving to me to meet him up the hill.

I waited for Christian to finish out the drive and then descended to the ground to join him to look for Corwin. We found him standing hopeful and excited on a gas well road. He said he had hit a small doe and had seen good blood. To me "good blood" means a lot of it, but to Corwin's inexperienced eyes any red liquid was sufficient. We located the four or five drops of blood Corwin had found and then searched for any other sign, but there was none.

I quizzed Corwin a couple of times on the deer's action after he'd taken the shot. He described how it seemed to trot off a little "humped," which, to me, was a clue that he had gut shot the doe. With that, the three of us spread out and began our search through the goldenrod and barren apple trees. Christian followed a wide path, and a few minutes later I heard him yell that he'd found the arrow. I hopefully asked if it was stuck in a deer, but his reply was negative. My hopes were dashed.

We inspected the arrow first by sight. There was good, clear blood from tip to fletching, a sign that Corwin had managed a complete pass through. On the tip there was white hair and some fat, not a good sign because the belly hair of a deer is white. Then I put my nose to the arrow as a test and didn't like what I found: the sour, rank smell of gut. Not good. From one end to the other, the arrow had the dreaded smell of the inside of a deer's food-burning machine. Not a pleasant odor to say the least. Now I knew we were dealing with a deer that could suffer for a few days before dying. Not good. The problem was that we didn't have a lot of time for tracking.

After searching for an hour or so, we gave up and moved on disappointed in not getting the meat and for leaving an animal in distress. It's hard for me to lose my own deer but much harder to watch my son feeling the pain of his moment of triumph turning into disaster. Finally, with a ton of reluctance, we headed back to where we were staying. On the way, we stopped to drown our sorrows with some hot food and the warm atmosphere of a little diner nationally famous for its hot dogs. It helped a little, but the sting of the lost deer didn't go away.

Wednesday morning proved to be too cold for sitting in a treestand. We slept in and packed our gear in our vehicle for the trip home. I couldn't get Corwin's deer off my mind, and I felt the need to relieve our hurting hearts by one more search. I knew there was a chance the wounded deer had survived the cold night. Deer will often go downhill to a water source to wait and heal up, and that was an area we hadn't completely searched. So we headed back to the woods.

I set Christian up on watch in case we flushed out a buck during our search. As Corwin and I trudged the creek bottom, I knew that looking for the doe was like looking for a dime in a football stadium filled with people. We gave it a good try, but with no results we left the creek bottom. As we headed uphill, I looked up toward our last slim chance. Above us was a plantation of thick, nearly impassable evergreen trees. A deer could hide in there for weeks and we would never find it. I instructed Corwin to crawl through, if needed, as this was our last hope of finding his wounded deer. I tried several times to penetrate the thick brush in the woods and had to resort to crawling in. Only if I bent completely over could I make my way through parts of it. From my knees I could look down between the rows, but I couldn't see or hear Corwin.

As I approached the top half of the woods, I set my mind to face Corwin's disappointment once again. I felt the slap and scratch of branches on my face and body. All at once one of the sweetest sounds a hunter-dad could ever hear reached my thankful ears.

"I found my deer, Daddy!" Corwin's excited voice came rolling through the mass of scraggly branches. "I'm coming, Corwin!" I yelled back.

I found myself not caring at all about the sharp branches that tore at me. Ahead lay the prize we so longed to see. I had to stop a few times to get a bead on Corwin's location. At last there he was with a grin as big as my own 28 years earlier when I'd dropped my first deer.

Corwin's deer was a yearling, a perfect, tender, table-meat doe that any young bow hunter could be proud of. We all agreed that the next morning, after a good night's sleep, we would honor the life of the animal by enjoying one of our favorite dishes that venison can yield: a simple and easy breakfast of fried backstrap and eggs.

Corwin easily dragged his young prize up the hill to the road. Rites of passage come in many forms, and in our family one rite is field dressing the first deer, with some help from Dad, of course. Corwin did a great job.

Our ride home was an exercise in telling, retelling, and telling again the story of the one that almost got away. The sweetest part was that after many years of watching and wishing, Corwin at last added his name to the elite list of hunters who have taken a deer with a bow and arrow.

Curt's Healthy Breakfast Backstraps

½ venison backstrap (approximately 7 inches)
¼ stick butter
1 large onion, chopped
3 to 4 large cloves garlic

Slice the backstrap into ¼-inch strips.

In a skillet, melt the butter and add the venison. Cook on medium to high heat. Add the onion and garlic. Cook until the red no longer shows in the center of meat. (Be careful not to overcook.)

Tip: Serve with eggs and toast. With a quick, simple breakfast, timing is everything. Be sure you start with the meat about 1½ minutes before you put the bread in the toaster and start the eggs. With that plan, everything should be done at the same time.

Tip: To avoid fighting over the tasty backstrap, the first and last piece should always go to the one who took the shot and provided the venison.

"On the Run" Backstraps

by Dave Quick

> 2 lbs. venison backstrap
> Italian vinegar and oil salad dressing or marinade
> salt

This recipe is super simple and great for folks like us—grandparents of nine grandkids and always on the go. Using a good-sized venison backstrap, cut sections about 3 inches thick. Trim so all you have is nice red meat. Then treat like you would butterfly chops, by cutting down the middle, leaving about 1 inch at the bottom. Fold your "chop" over on the cutting board, creating a thick steak.

Pound the steaks with a meat hammer to tenderize. I find this works very well with larger or older deer.

Place your steaks in a large ziplock bag, keeping them separated as much as possible even as they lie nice and flat in the bag. Pour in the Italian dressing and perhaps a teaspoon or so of salt. Be sure the dressing is on both sides of the meat in the bag. Now, lay the bag flat on the counter and squeeze out the air as you carefully zip the bag closed. Fold the bag up until you have a nice, compact package. Place in the fridge overnight.

When ready to cook, start a charcoal fire and allow it to get glowing-red hot. However, moderation is the key here. Do not use too much charcoal.

You will close the vents on the grill once the meat is on to reduce the heat. Sear the meat at first, but after that only turn the meat once. Watch the temperature, keeping it modest. Be careful not to overcook the steaks. They should have just a hint of pink in the center when done.

Serve with green beans and mashed potatoes. This is super fast and easy when you're in a hurry yet still want a tasty and convenient meal.

Dave Quick, friend, fellow hunter, and wild game cook

Grandpa's Venison Backstrap

1½ cups saltines	pepper (or McCormick's Seasoning
3 eggs	Salt)
½ cup milk	1 venison backstrap
1 tsp. salt	½ cup vegetable oil

In a flat dish, crush the crackers.

In a bowl, whisk the eggs, milk, salt, and pepper.

Cut the venison backstrap into butterfly chops, approximately ¼-inch thick on each half. Cover each butterfly chop in the cracker crumbs and dredge in the egg mixture. Cover again with cracker crumbs and place on a large dish.

Once ready, place backstrap in a large skillet with vegetable oil. Cook 3 minutes or so per side over medium heat until desired doneness.

SOUL FOOD
He who dwells in the shelter of the Most High will abide in the shadow of the Almighty (Psalm 91:1).

Venison Roast with Soup

3 to 4 lbs. venison roast	1 medium onion, chopped,
seasoning salt	or 2 T. onion flakes
1 10.5-oz. can cream of mushroom	2 to 4 medium-sized carrots
soup	2 to 4 medium potatoes
1 10.5-oz. can cream of celery soup	2 cups water
1 32-oz. container beef broth	

Rub the roast with seasoning salt and place in a baking pan with a lid. Spoon in cream of mushroom and cream of celery soups. Add beef broth and onion.

Cut carrots and potatoes into bite-sized pieces and add to pan. Add water and mix everything well.

Cover pan and bake at 325° for 3 hours.

Serve the soup, carrots, and potatoes in a bowl and the meat on a plate. (The soup has a wonderful consistency, and the soup and meat taste great!)

PART 1: BIG GAME

BIG GAME

Venison Tenderloin Celebration

2 venison tenderloins
2 cups mushrooms, cut or whole

1 stick butter or margarine

Optional
onions, diced or chopped
salt

Cut the venison tenderloins into thin, bite-sized strips.

In a wok or heavy skillet, heat the butter to a relatively high temperature. Place the tenderloins in the wok and brown, approximately 2 minutes. (Don't overcook or the meat will turn tough.)

Add the mushrooms to the wok. If desired, add onions and salt. Continue stirring for two minutes or so, turn off the heat. Cover the wok with the lid or foil and allow contents to steam for approximately 5 minutes.

SOUL FOOD
*Like arrows in the hand of a warrior, so are the children of one's youth.
How blessed is the man whose quiver is full of them* (Psalm 127:4-5).

Venison Barbecue Stir-fry

2 venison steaks
1 cup barbecue sauce
½ T. vegetable oil

2 cups mixed stir-fry vegetables
1 4-oz. can cut mushrooms in liquid
1 cup instant rice

Cut venison steaks into stir-fry sized chunks. Marinate in the barbecue sauce for a few hours or coat the meat for immediate use.

Heat the wok or heavy skillet to cooking temperature and add vegetable oil. Quickly brown the venison, and then turn down the heat slightly. Add the cut mushrooms with liquid and the stir-fry vegetables. If your wok has a dome lid, put the lid in place and allow to steam for 5 minutes.

Prepare the rice according to package instructions.

Serve the stir-fry over the cooked rice.

Tip: This is a great recipe for a fast-paced lifestyle. The barbecue sauce adds a delightful flavor.

Sliced Venison Roast with Mushroom Gravy

1 14.5-oz. can cut green beans
1 7.3-oz. can cut mushrooms
1 lb. venison roast
3 strips of bacon

1 10.5-oz. can cream of mushroom
soup
8 oz. milk
1 cup flour

Cook the green beans. Drain and save the liquid.

Drain and save the liquid from the mushrooms.

Using a liquid injector, inject the liquid from the green beans and mushrooms into the roast. Wrap the roast with three strips of bacon and secure with toothpicks. Place roast in a roasting pan.

Cook at 300° for approximately 2 hours, until the center temperature is 170°.

Take the roaster out of the oven, and pour the green beans into the liquid in the bottom of the roaster. Let the roast and green beans rest.

In a saucepan, mix the cream of mushroom soup with the milk. Stir in the cut mushrooms. Add the flour and mix well. Heat until thick and hot.

Cut the roast into thin slices on the bias. Ladle the gravy over the meat and serve.

Tip: Serve with Half Runner Green Beans (page 207) and Fireplace Baked Potatoes (page 214).

Quick Family Venison Stew

1 lb. venison
4 medium potatoes, cut into pieces
3 medium onions, diced
4 to 6 large carrots, thinly sliced

3 stalks celery, thinly sliced
1 32-oz. container beef broth
4 T. ketchup

Cut the venison into bite-sized chunks and place in a Crock-Pot. Add the potatoes, onions, carrots, and celery. Pour in the beef broth and enough water to cover everything. Add ketchup and mix everything well.

Let the stew simmer on medium for 6 to 8 hours.

Tip: This is an especially good recipe for tough cuts of meat, such as neck and shoulder.

Venison Stew for Canning

2 quarts venison, canned
1 32-oz. container beef broth
2 10.5-oz. cans cream of celery soup
4 to 5 medium potatoes, chunked
   w/skin or peeled

2 medium onions, diced
6 T. ketchup
salt

In a large pan with a lid, combine all ingredients. (You can add water to thicken or thin stew to the desired consistency.) Bring to a boil, and then reduce heat. Simmer for 2 to 3 hours until meat becomes tender. Remove from heat.

Wash and prepare canning jars. Have lids ready according to canning directions.

Add salt to the jars at the rate of ¼ tsp. per pint (½ tsp. per quart).

Ladle hot stew into jars, put on and adjust lids according to canning directions, and install rings. Place in pressure canner. Process quarts at 10 lbs. for 1 hour 30 minutes or pints for 1 hour 15 minutes.

Remove jars and set on several layers of dish towels to cool. Inspect lids for tight seal. Label and store.

Tips for Canning Venison or Elk

Having canned venison on the shelf and at the ready is a great way to be ready for quick meals because you can just open, heat, and serve.

Consult a canning book for specific directions, but here are some tips to make the canning go more smoothly.

- Cut venison into bite-sized squares. Remove all fat and as much membrane as possible. (If you prefer, you can precook the meat prior to canning, which makes even quicker meal preparation possible. Consult your canning book for instructions.)

- According to canning directions, clean the desired number of pint or quart canning jars. (I recommend doing 4 to 5 quarts at a time.)

- Add one teaspoon of salt to each jar, followed by a small amount of boiling water. (I prefer to dissolve the salt this way before packing the meat.)

- Add venison to jars and top off with boiling water, leaving the amount of headspace recommended in canning directions.

- Process venison according to the canning directions for beef.

- Be sure to follow the specific directions that came with your pressure cooker.

Venison Barbecue Tenderloin Meal

2 venison tenderloins
4 T. ketchup
1½ T. barbecue sauce

2 baking potatoes
vegetable of your choice

Take two venison tenderloins and place in covered pan, along with enough water to cover meat. Add ketchup and barbecue sauce.

Bring to boil and then reduce heat. Simmer for 2 to 3 hours or until the meat is "fall apart tender."

Bake or mash potatoes and prepare the vegetables.

Enjoy!

Tip: This recipe works well with other tender cuts of venison, such as back-strap cut into tenderloin-sized strips or other rump or hindquarter cuts.

Dave's Venison Stroganoff

1 lb. venison tenderloin or steak,
    ½-inch thick
2 T. butter or margarine
½ lb. mushrooms, sliced
½ cup onion, diced
1 10.5-oz. can condensed beef broth

2 T. ketchup
1 clove garlic, diced
1 T. salt
3 to 4 cups noodles, cooked
3 T. flour
1 cup sour cream

Cut venison into ½-inch cubes.

Melt butter in skillet. Add mushrooms and onion, cooking and stirring until onion is tender. Remove from skillet.

In the same skillet, cook meat until light brown. Stir in beef broth, ketch-up, garlic, and salt.

Cover and simmer for 15 minutes.

Prepare noodles per package instructions.

Blend flour into meat mixture. Add mushrooms and onions. Heat to boil-ing, stirring constantly. Boil and stir 1 minute. Reduce heat. Add sour cream and continue stirring until well mixed. Serve over noodles.

Venison Rigatoni

rigatoni
1 quart jar of canned venison

1 can cream of mushroom soup

In a large pan, boil the rigatoni. Drain.

In a separate pan, prepare cream of mushroom soup according to the directions.

Open jar of venison, drain, and rinse. Add the venison to the soup and let simmer.

That is all there is to it! Ladle the soup and venison over the rigatoni and serve piping hot, along with your choice of side dishes. This is a great recipe to use when you don't have much time to spend cooking.

SOUL FOOD

*We know that God causes all things to work together for good
to those who love God, to those who are called according to His purpose*
(Romans 8:28).

Venison d'Paprika

2 to 2.5 lbs. venison, 1-inch cubes	2 medium onions, chopped
1½ cups flour	2 to 3 cloves garlic, minced
2 tsp. paprika	1 tsp. marjoram (or Italian seasoning)
dash of salt	1 29-oz. can diced tomatoes
pinch of pepper	2 cups water
3 to 4 T. oil	1 cup red wine (or beef broth)

Optional
1 cup sour cream

Roll venison cubes in flour seasoned with 1 teaspoon paprika, salt, and pepper.

Heat oil in heavy Dutch oven or cast-iron skillet. Over medium-high heat, brown floured cubes a few at a time. (If you crowd the pan with the cubes, they will steam instead of brown.) Remove to a warm dish after they've cooked.

After meat is browned, cook onions in same skillet over medium heat until browned. Add garlic, remaining paprika, marjoram, tomatoes, water, and wine.

Cover and simmer for 20 minutes.

Add browned meat, stir, and cook over low heat for 2 hours.

Optional: Just before serving, add sour cream.

Tip: Serve over noodles, rice, or Texas toast.

SOUL FOOD
The LORD sustains all who fall and raises up all who are bowed down. The eyes of all look to You, and You give them their food in due time (Psalm 145:14-15).

Uncle Bob's Venison Loaf

4 dashes of Tabasco	3 or 4 cloves garlic, crushed
1/3 cup V8 juice	pinch of oregano
1½ lbs. ground venison	1 T. butter
1/3 cup applesauce	salt
1 medium onion, diced	pepper
2 medium to large carrots, shredded	8 soda crackers, finely crushed

Add Tabasco to the V8 juice. In a large mixing bowl, combine the V8 juice, venison, and applesauce.

Sauté onion, carrots, garlic, and oregano in a cast-iron fry pan with butter until onions are translucent. Sprinkle lightly with salt and generously with pepper while sautéing.

Combine onion mixture and crushed crackers with venison mixture and mix everything thoroughly.

Pack mixture firmly into a well-buttered 8½ x 4½ x 2½-inch baking dish. Bake at 350° for 1 hour.

Venison Patties

1½ lbs. ground venison	1 medium onion, finely chopped
1 lb. ground breakfast sausage	½ tsp. soy sauce (per patty)
bacon strips (1 per patty)	

Mix venison, sausage, and onion. Form into patties about 4 inches across and 1 inch thick. Wrap bacon around edge of each patty and pin with a toothpick where it overlaps.

Sear both sides of meat in hot skillet, and then reduce to low heat. Turn occasionally, and after turning several times, put soy sauce on each patty. Cook until meat attains desired doneness or the thermometer reads 160°.

Tip: Serve with Broccoli Cauliflower Salad (see page 210).

SOUL FOOD

The plans of the heart belong to man, but the answer of the tongue is from the LORD. All the ways of a man are clean in his own sight, but the LORD weighs the motives (Proverbs 16:1).

Pat's Venison Crock-Pot Stew

2 lbs. venison, cut into bite-sized
   pieces
Italian salad dressing (enough to
   cover and marinate meat)
½ lb. bacon
1 medium onion, chopped
1 pkg. dry onion soup mix
1 14.5-oz. can new potatoes

2 cups baby carrots, peeled
1 T. black pepper
1 tsp. salt
1 T. garlic powder
1 7.3-oz. jar mushroom pieces
1 10.5-oz. can cream of mushroom
   soup

Optional
1 cup celery

brown rice

Marinate venison in Italian salad dressing for at least 2 hours.

Line bottom of Crock-Pot with half the bacon. Place venison in Crock-Pot and cover with remaining bacon strips. Add the onion on top of the bacon. Now dump in the dry onion soup mix. Add potatoes and carrots. Add pepper, salt, and garlic powder. Add the mushroom pieces and then the mushroom soup.

Cook on low for 5 to 6 hours. Do not stir or mix up.

Prepare brown rice per package instructions.

Ladle venison mixture over brown rice and serve.

SOUL FOOD

*Many, O Lord my God, are the wonders which You have done,
and Your thoughts toward us; there is none to compare with You.
If I would declare and speak of them, they would be too
numerous to count* (Psalm 40:5).

Venison Butterfly Chops

1 egg	½ cup peanut oil
½ cup milk	6 strips bacon
4 venison loin chops	2 T. cooking oil from bacon
1 cup flour	

Gravy

2 cups milk	2 T. oil from wok (for the bacon and
¼ cup plus 1 T. all-purpose flour	meat flavors)

Beat egg and add milk. Set aside.

Butterfly venison loin chops and dredge them in flour. Dip them in the egg/milk mixture and dredge in flour again.

In a wok or heavy skillet, heat peanut oil and fry several strips of bacon until crisp. Remove the bacon and dry thoroughly on a paper towel. (Using a wok helps because the heat is high and it browns the outside of the chops quickly, sealing in the juices.)

Place the butterflied chops in the same cooking oil the bacon just came out of and deep-fat fry until desired doneness.

While the chops are cooking, make gravy. Combine milk, flour, and 2 tablespoons of cooking oil from the pan.

Serve the gravy over the chops, and crumble the bacon over the gravy.

Tip: Butterfly a chop by cutting it down the middle, leaving about 1 inch at the bottom. Fold the chop over on the cutting board, creating a nice thick steak.

SOUL FOOD

Everyone who partakes only of milk is not accustomed to the word of righteousness, for he is an infant. But solid food is for the mature, who because of practice have their senses trained to discern good and evil (Hebrews 5:13-14).

Venison Cutlets

venison cutlets, cut into 4-inch squares and ½-inch thick

Marinade

½ cup soy sauce
½ cup lemon juice

¼ cup Worcestershire sauce

Cooking Ingredients

bacon (1 slice per cutlet)
1 cup flour

nonstick cooking spray

Put venison cutlets in a ziplock bag.

Combine marinade ingredients and pour over meat in the ziplock bag. Marinate for 2 to 3 hours.

Remove meat from marinade and wrap each cutlet edge with a slice of bacon, pinning it with a toothpick.

Roll meat in flour and brown in hot skillet coated with nonstick cooking spray. Remove from heat and put in a baking pan.

Bake covered at 350° for 1 hour.

Poor Man's "Veal-ison"

Here's a recipe an old-timer gave me years ago. When you butcher a deer, cut the steaks very thin: ⅜ inches or less. Freeze them until ready to cook (always freeze before cooking). Allow the steaks to thaw in a pan of whole milk in the refrigerator. (Never thaw venison at room temperature.)

1 egg, beaten	1 tsp. garlic powder
¼ cup milk	1 cup bread crumbs, seasoned
1 lb. venison steaks	3 T. butter (or 2 T. olive oil)

Make egg batter by combining the egg and milk. Dip steaks in the batter.

If desired, sprinkle garlic powder on bread crumbs. Now roll the steaks in the bread crumbs.

Fry in butter and/or olive oil.

Tip: You'll be pleasantly surprised at how similar to veal this tastes. Serve with rice or potato and vegetable.

Venison Steak with Bacon

1 venison steak, about 1 inch thick	3 strips bacon

Take any size venison steak and wrap with 2 to 3 strips of bacon, pinning the bacon on with wooden toothpicks. The bacon tenderizes the steaks while adding delicious flavor.

Broil steaks until bacon is crispy. Let steak rest for 10 minutes before serving.

SOUL FOOD

A worker's appetite works for him, for his hunger urges him on
(Proverbs 16:26).

Dutch Oven Venison Stew

3 lb. venison, cubed
2 T. cooking oil
1 32-oz. can of beef broth
1 tsp. salt
1 cup water
4 carrots, diced (or 1 quart canned
   carrots)

2 medium onions, chopped
4 large potatoes, cubed
other vegetables, such as peas,
   corn, green beans

In an uncovered Dutch oven hung from a tripod over a wood fire, brown venison in cooking oil. Add beef broth, salt, and water.

Cover and cook 30 minutes.

Add carrots and onions, and cook for 30 minutes.

Add potatoes and any other vegetables desired, and cook for another 30 minutes.

SOUL FOOD

*"I know the plans that I have for you," declares the LORD,
"plans for welfare and not for calamity to give you a future
and a hope. Then you will call upon Me and come and pray
to Me, and I will listen to you. You will seek Me and find Me
when you search for Me with all your heart. And I will
be found by you," declares the LORD*
(Jeremiah 29:11-14).

Barbecued Deer Ribs

Sauce

2½ cups water
3 cups ketchup
1 T. white vinegar (if venison may be
    a bit gamy, increase to 3 T.)
¼ cup lemon juice
½ cup Worcestershire sauce

½ cup pure maple syrup
½ to 1 cup brown sugar
2 medium onions, diced
2 T. chili powder
½ tsp. salt

Ribs

6 lbs. venison ribs with some loin
    meat attached

black pepper, freshly ground
salt

Preheat oven to 325°.

Sauce

In large bowl, combine all sauce ingredients. Blend well. Taste sauce and, if desired, add up to ½ cup more brown sugar.

Ribs

Sprinkle ribs with pepper and additional salt. Double layer in 5-quart roasting pan, and roast for 1 hour.

Remove ribs from oven and pour sauce over them. Put back in oven, increase heat to 350°, and bake until ribs just begin to char on top, approximately 1½ hours.

Turn ribs over, cover pan, and bake 30 minutes longer or until ribs are tender and sauce is thick.

To serve, place ribs on platter and cover with sauce.

SOUL FOOD

From the rising of the sun to its setting the name of the LORD
is to be praised (Psalm 113:3).

Venison Steaks in Italian Dressing

| 5 venison steaks, cut thin | Italian dressing, enough to cover meat |

Place four or five thinly cut venison steaks or butterflied backstraps in a large ziplock bag. Fill bag with Italian dressing, enough to cover meat. Refrigerate for 24 hours, turning occasionally.

Remove meat from marinade and cook slowly over a fire of mesquite, walnut, or Spanish oak. Nut, fruit, or berry wood works well also.

SOUL FOOD

How blessed is he whose transgression is forgiven, whose sin is covered! How blessed is the man to whom the LORD does not impute iniquity, and in whose spirit there is no deceit! (Psalm 32:1-2).

Scrumptious Venison Hors d'oeuvres

by Preston Mayo, submitted by LaBreeska Hemphill

2 lbs. venison tenderloins	8 oz. cream cheese
ice water (enough to cover meat)	jalapenos, sliced
2 tsp. salt	8 oz. bacon slices, halved

Soak tenderloins in ice water and salt for 1 hour. Rinse very well to remove salt.

On each piece of raw steak place 1 teaspoon cream cheese. Top with 1 slice of jalapeno and wrap with half a slice of bacon. Pin together with a wooden toothpick.

Place on grill and cook until bacon is crispy and tenderloins reach 160°.

SOUL FOOD

I would have despaired unless I had believed that I would see the goodness of the LORD in the land of the living. Wait for the LORD; be strong and let your heart take courage; yes, wait for the LORD (Psalm 27:13-14).

Louisiana Deer Chili

by James Mayo, submitted by LaBreeska Hemphill

2 lbs. ground venison
2 T. olive oil
1 onion, chopped
salt
2 T. flour
1 10-oz. can Rotel tomatoes (diced tomatoes and green chilies)

1 15-oz. can diced tomatoes
1 15-oz. can tomato sauce
2 cups water
5 T. chili powder
1 cup whole milk

Optional
1 15-oz. can of black beans or chili beans

Brown meat in olive oil with onion and salt to taste. Drain.

Add remaining ingredients except milk and cook for 20 minutes.

Add milk and cook for 10 more minutes.

This is fast, easy, and delicious!

SOUL FOOD

*The fear of the LORD is clean, enduring forever; the judgments
of the LORD are true; they are righteous altogether. They are more
desirable than gold, yes, than much fine gold; sweeter also
than honey and the drippings of the honeycomb*
(Psalm 19:9-10).

Dangerous Deer Dander

OF ALL THE EXPERIENCES I'VE HAD AS A DEER HUNTER, hardly any compare to what happened one late-September morning several years ago. The emotions I felt were some of the highest and some of the lowest…rather, I should say some of the scariest I've experienced.

My son, Nathan, and I got on our deer stands before daylight. We were relatively close to each other, and I was excited for both of us. It was Nathan's first time in the woods with archery equipment, and I was yet to connect to a deer with my compound bow. The woods we were in held great promise for at least one of us getting off a good shot. Needless to say, I was on the edge of my climber seat as the sun peeked over the horizon.

As it turned out, that morning we both got our first kills with a bow and arrow. Nathan's was a plump doe, and I downed what I thought was a doe but found out when I recovered it that it was a good-sized button buck. Without a doubt, the fact that both of us had shared such an incredible accomplishment on the same morning provided a memory we will always treasure. But that's not where the dynamics of emotion ends.

After I found my kill, I headed to the truck to wait for Nathan to join me. When I exited the woods and looked across the field toward where I'd parked, I saw Nathan sitting on the ground, leaning against the right front driver's side tire. From a distance it looked as though he was resting. As I walked closer, I saw that he wasn't resting at all. He was trying to breathe! His lips were a pale blue, his breathing was shallow, and he barely responded when I knelt in front of him and spoke. I was baffled by his condition, but my immediate assessment was that he looked like he was having an allergic reaction to something. But what?

Nathan was around 14 at the time. When he was younger, we found out through a few overnight stays with babysitters and friends who had cats that he had an allergy to the critters' dander. The simple solution to that dilemma was to keep cats away from him. Had he found a stray and played with it while at the truck? And then it hit me! The culprit had to be deer dander.

I quickly stood up and circled the truck. There it was. He had connected with his doe and drug it the 200 yards to the truck. The combination of a relatively warm September morning and handling the deer had created a medical emergency.

I quickly turned the truck engine on, turned the air conditioner on to maximum cool, went back to Nathan and wrestled his oxygen-starved body into the cab. I got in on my side and took off for home...and to the medicine cabinet that held the Benadryl. Thankfully, the clean, cold air provided Nathan with some immediate relief, but the drive of nearly 20 miles seemed like forever for both of us. By the time we got home, Nathan was almost breathing normally. Once we got into the house and put some medicine into his system, he returned to his regular young self.

I was completely surprised that deer dander can cause the same reaction as cat dander. And Nathan is not alone in his allergy. I've discovered since then that another friend's son had experienced the same response to deer dander. My friend and I discussed our sons' unusual struggle and managed a respectful chuckle at the thought that it was our boys' ploy to feign deer dander allergy so that their respective "old man" would do all the dragging after their shots were taken.

Eventually Nathan and I figured out that the colder the weather, the less effect deer dander had. For that reason, Nathan prefers to hunt in the colder months of the year.

By the way, you probably noted I left two deer lying on the ground when I loaded Nathan into the truck and rushed home. The good news is that after Annie and I were sure he was going to be okay, she took over his care and suggested I hurry back to the farm to retrieve our trophies. Thankfully, the meat was still good. Nathan and I enjoyed a bit of satisfaction when we consumed Annie's Famous Venison Chili that contained meat from the doe that had caused both of us such a scare.

Nathan Chapman

Annie's Famous Venison Chili

2 lbs. ground venison	1 28-oz. can of tomatoes
1 large onion, chopped	1 28-oz. can of pinto beans
2 packets McCormick's Mild Chili Seasoning	

Brown the meat and onion in a large skillet. Drain all fat. (I've even put the cooked meat in a colander and rinsed it off with hot water to get more fat off.)

Add the chili seasoning to the meat, stirring until mixed thoroughly. Add tomatoes and beans.

Simmer on low for at least 45 minutes. (The longer the better.)

Tip: Serve with Cornbread (see page 222).

Venison Roast

5 lbs. venison roast	1 10.5-oz. can cream of mushroom
¼ tsp. black pepper	soup
1 pkg. dry onion soup mix	½ tsp. garlic powder

Place the venison roast on a large sheet of heavy-duty aluminum foil. Cover meat with remaining ingredients, and wrap foil securely around everything to seal in heat and juices.

Bake at 350° degrees for 4½ hours. Let set for 20 minutes before slicing so the juices will settle.

SOUL FOOD

*Now to Him who is able to do far more abundantly beyond
all that we ask or think, according to the power that works
within us, to Him be the glory in the church and in Christ Jesus
to all generations forever and ever. Amen*
(Ephesians 3:20-21).

Venison Lasagna

8 oz. lasagna noodles
2 lbs. ground venison
1 medium onion, chopped
1 32-oz. jar spaghetti sauce
2 cups sour cream

2 cups cottage cheese
½ lb. cheddar cheese, shredded (or
    another type of cheese)
Parmesan cheese

Cook noodles according to package directions and set aside.

In a skillet, brown the venison and onion. Drain off fat. Add spaghetti sauce to the meat mixture and heat thoroughly.

In a large bowl, mix the sour cream and cottage cheese together.

Layer the ingredients in a casserole dish: noodles, meat sauce, sour cream mixture. Repeat the layers, ending with meat on top. Cover the top layer of meat with shredded cheese and sprinkle on Parmesan cheese.

Bake at 350° for 45 minutes or until the meat is bubbling and the cheese is nice and brown.

SOUL FOOD

A voice came to him, "Get up, Peter, kill and eat!" But Peter said, "By no means, Lord, for I have never eaten anything unholy and unclean." Again a voice came to him a second time, "What God has cleansed, no longer consider unholy"
(Acts 10:13-15).

Nine Mile Venison Sloppy Joes

2 lbs. ground venison
22-oz. bottle of salsa
2 10-oz. cans tomato soup, undiluted

2 T. brown sugar (or molasses)
1 green pepper, chopped
hamburger buns

In a large, heavy skillet, brown the ground venison until it is no longer pink. Drain the fat. Stir in the remaining ingredients and simmer for 20 minutes or until heated thoroughly.

Serve on hamburger buns.

Tip: Serve Coleslaw (page 208) on top of the sloppy joes—a West Virginia custom.

Roasted Venison Tenderloin

2 lbs. potatoes, quartered	2 tsp. dried rosemary
1 lb. carrots, sliced on the diagonal	salt
1 large onion, cut into chunks	pepper
2 T. canola oil	dash of Mrs. Dash seasoning
2 lbs. venison tenderloin	3 T. butter, melted

Prepare the vegetables and mix them together in a large bowl. Add 1 table-spoon canola oil and stir. Make sure all the vegetables are covered in oil.

In a heavy skillet, fry the tenderloin in 1 tablespoon canola oil until the meat is just brown.

Put the meat in a roasting pan or casserole dish. Place the veggies around the meat and sprinkle them with the seasonings. Drizzle melted butter over the meat and vegetables.

Cover and roast at 450° for 45 minutes. Remove the cover and roast for another 20 minutes, allowing the potatoes to brown.

SOUL FOOD

Many are saying, "Who will show us any good?" Lift up the light of Your countenance upon us, O LORD! You have put gladness in my heart, more than when their grain and new wine abound. In peace I will both lie down and sleep, for You alone, O LORD, make me to dwell in safety (Psalm 4:6-8).

Beginner's Venison Stew

2 to 3 lbs. venison, cut into cubes	2 T. Worcestershire sauce
4 T. olive oil	1 envelop dry onion soup mix
1 T. kosher salt (kosher salt is purer and more coarse than table salt)	2 tsp. garlic, minced
	4 medium potatoes, quartered
pepper	6 carrots, sliced on the diagonal
6 cups water	4 stalks of celery, chopped
2 T. beef bouillon, granular or cubes	3 T. cornstarch

Rinse venison in cold water and pat dry. In a heavy pot or Dutch oven, heat the oil on medium high. Salt and pepper the meat cubes, and then brown the meat in the hot oil. Add the water, bouillon, Worcestershire sauce, dry soup mix, and garlic.

Simmer for 1½ hours.

Add potatoes, carrots, and celery and continue to simmer until the vegetables are tender.

Just before serving, remove ½ cup of broth and mix it with the cornstarch, making sure there are no lumps. Stir the mixture back into the meat and vegetables and simmer until the broth is thick. (You can add a little milk or a bit more beef broth if you need to thin the gravy.)

SOUL FOOD

For You formed my inward parts; You wove me in my mother's womb. I will give thanks to You, for I am fearfully and wonderfully made; wonderful are Your works, and my soul knows it very well
(Psalm 139:13-14).

A HUNTER'S PROMISE

I, beside the quiet doe,
Kneel and for a minute mourn
Between my victory and her woe
My quickly beating heart is torn.

High on this mountain midst the oaks
I vow to this beast that once had life
We will give thanks when down below
We taste your strength...your sacrifice.

ELK

The Test Is in the Tasting

IN THE LATE 1990S, MY SON, NATHAN, AND I went to Montana to hunt the mighty elk with guide and outfitter Randy Petrich. Annie was aware of the amount of family funds the adventure would cost us, and as the time drew near for Nathan and me to head west, I offered my best economic consolation to my dear wife. "Babe, can you really put a price tag on the value of making such memories with our son?" She nodded her head in agreement. (I had my turn to nod my head and keep my trap shut when she and Heidi took a trip to the historic town of Savannah, Georgia, a few weeks after Nathan and I returned from Montana.)

Thankfully, during the hunt Nathan and I were blessed with 6 x 6 bulls. We couldn't wait to get home and tell our tales. What made the homecoming even more special was that due to the relaxed luggage restrictions in air travel at the time, we brought both sets of antlers with us as checked baggage. We were the envy of every hunter who happened to be in the claim area when the baggage handlers brought them to us. The rest of the elk would be delivered in ten days or so (with an added cost of well over $200 for shipping).

Finally, the nearly 300 pounds of freezer-ready elk meat came to our door packed in dry ice. Annie thawed a package and used it that night as the main ingredient in her Easy Elk Stroganoff. Our family of four sat down to experience our very first meal of elk. Nathan and I were on pins and needles waiting for Annie to do the honors of taking the first taste. As she did, we wondered what she'd say. There's no way to describe the beauty of the words that came from her mouth after she slid her napkin across her lips. Perhaps a blazing red sunset behind Dexter Mountain where we took the elk might have come close to comparing with the beauty of her statement. "Boys..." She paused long enough to make us feel even more anticipation. "Boys, you're gonna have to go back and get another one. This elk is great!"

Annie smiled as Nathan and I high-fived each other. Heidi concurred with her mama's assessment of the tasty elk, and we high-fived again. Nathan and I had no trouble at all making plans to fulfill Annie's request.

Annie's Easy Elk Stroganoff

1 12-oz. pkg. egg noodles	8 oz. milk (or water)
1 lb. ground elk	2 T. Worcestershire sauce
1 large onion, chopped	8 oz. sour cream
1 10.5-oz. can cream of mushroom soup	

Prepare egg noodles according to package instructions.

Crumble meat into a skillet and add the chopped onion. Brown and drain, removing as much grease as possible. Then add the cream of mushroom soup and milk to the meat in the skillet. Pour in the Worcestershire sauce.

After heating thoroughly, add sour cream. Continue to simmer a bit longer to let flavors mingle, being careful to not allow mixture to boil.

Serve over the cooked noodles.

Tip: Family and friends who shy away from eating wild game will like this dish!

Elk Roast

3 to 5 lbs. elk meat (or deer, antelope, caribou)	1 pkg. dry beefy onion soup mix
1 10.5-oz can cream of mushroom soup	water

Place meat in medium roaster. Add both soup mixes with enough water to almost cover the meat.

Cover with roaster lid and bake for 3 to 4 hours, until meat is done and tender.

Serve immediately or it's even better the next day as leftovers. To set aside for the next day, let the mixture cool, slice the meat, and place in a large casserole dish. Cover with the gravy and refrigerate overnight. Reheat to serve.

Tip: Serve with Broccoli and Cauliflower Coleslaw (page 208).

Poor Man's Elk Steak

1 cup cracker crumbs, finely crushed
1 cup milk, cold
3 lbs. ground elk
salt to taste
pepper to taste

1 cup flour
3 T. butter
1 10.5-oz. can cream of
  mushroom soup

Mix crackers and milk thoroughly. Add elk burger and salt and pepper to your taste.

Place approximately an inch thick in a flat dish. Refrigerate overnight.

The next day, cut into serving portions and roll in flour.

In a hot skillet, brown both sides of meat mixture patties in butter. Put in a baking dish and pour mushroom soup over all.

Bake at 350° for 1 hour.

SOUL FOOD

Forever, O Lord, Your word is settled in heaven. Your faithfulness continues throughout all generations; You established the earth, and it stands. They stand this day according to Your ordinances, for all things are Your servants (Psalm 119:89-91).

The Longest Night

IN MY LIFE I'VE HAD MY SHARE OF RESTLESS NIGHTS waiting to hear the results of something important to me. The nail-biting vigils have been for everything from a test score in high school to a diagnosis following a medical test, from finding out if my wife and I were approved for a home loan to discovering my name was drawn for a special hunting season. All these overnighters were tension-filled, but there is one that remains near the top of the list of most anxious waits. In this case, it involved a bull elk.

I was hunting with Rising Son Outfitter owner and guide Randy Petrich. The pursuit for elk during this hunt was with archery equipment. My friend and fellow bow hunter Eddy Richey joined us for a five-day quest. It was a Wednesday afternoon, around 5:45, when the action unexpectedly got hot.

We left Spike Camp on horseback close to three o'clock and headed down a long flat in the Gallatin National Forest. The plan was to slip along and do some bugling to connect with a lovesick bull. We stopped at a wallow to study the size of the hoofprints in the mud. We were sitting in our saddles when we heard a powerful bugle come from near the top of the mountain to our right. Randy said it sounded like a very mature bull. He decided to bugle back to see if he could get a response. When he blew his call, what happened next is somewhat of a blur.

Not more than 200 yards away to our left on the flat below us, a bull answered Randy's call. Our guide's eyes widened as he said, "Grab your bows and let's head downhill! He's closer now and sounds like a nice one!"

We hardly had time to hit the ground and gather around a huge pine when we heard the bull bugle again, closer this time—maybe 100 yards away. Eddy was lying on his side to minimize his profile. I was on my knees at Randy's left side, facing down the flat. Randy was also on his knees ready to repeat the cow call if needed.

Suddenly Randy spoke with an excited whisper: "He's coming in!" He looked at his two hunters to determine who could get the best shot. I was hoping Eddy would get the first shot, but Randy quickly noted that in his reclined position Eddy wouldn't have time to prepare to shoot. "Steve, knock an arrow. That bull's comin' in—and it's yours!"

In the pressure of the moment, my hands shook but I managed to click an arrow onto the string and attach the release. Then I saw the bull coming straight toward us. I thought he might walk right over us, but he turned broadside and stepped slowly behind some large trees. I judged the distance to be 35 yards or so.

I saw that the elk was looking down the trail in front of him and decided it was time to go to full draw. The problem was that I didn't have time to turn a little sideways to get some torque on the string like I usually do. Consequently, I had the bow straight out in front of me. I tugged with all my might, but I wasn't gaining any distance on pulling the string back. Plus, I was so rattled by the sudden encounter that all the techniques I'd practiced prior to the hunt got lost in my head. I looked for it, but couldn't find it. I realized that the string had turned to piano wire, and all my muscles had turned to wet noodles. I was in a real dilemma. A huge elk was in range, and I couldn't get to full draw!

As if another me arrived on the scene to talk me back into reality, I heard, "Don't be defeated, Steve! You can get the string in position. Just pull with everything in you. *Do it now!*" So I did! And as I did, the bow shook like Jell-O on a jackhammer. About two-thirds into my draw, I was shaking so badly the arrow jumped out of its rest and fell alongside the lower riser, but still connected by its knock to the string. I was embarrassed, to say the least, as I relaxed the limbs to recover the arrow.

Randy worriedly watched as I slowly lifted the arrow back up and placed it on the pronged rest. In those few short moments of rest for my arms, I must have regained a bit of strength because when I pulled the string back again I was surprised that I could feel the limbs yielding to my draw. Suddenly the compound bow system reached the break-over point. Instantly the pull weight dropped from 65 pounds to about 25 pounds. I was at full draw!

Amazingly, the bull was still there and had even halted. Randy said later that when the bow broke over I grunted rather loudly, and that's what stopped the bull in its tracks. For whatever reason, I was grateful to find the bull in my peep sight. But his vitals area was visible only through the forks of a tree. If I were going to take the shot, I would have to send the arrow precisely between the two trunks. There was no room for error.

I surveyed the situation for a few seconds and decided I could send the arrow safely between the forks of the tree. I also knew the bull wouldn't linger long. I settled in and felt surprisingly steady as I pressed the trigger on the release. The bow worked perfectly, and I watched the arrow sail precisely between the tree trunks and bury into the elk. What an accomplishment!

"Did you get him good?" Randy quizzed as the bull took off and headed downhill to the flat below us.

"I believe I did. The impact sounded good!"

Eddy added his assessment that gave us pause: "From where I'm lying, I could see the arrow penetrate up to the fletching. It was a good hit, but it wasn't a pass through."

Randy offered a subdued groan at the news that there probably wasn't an exit wound, which would have caused the bull to bleed freely and die quickly.

My joy turned to concern. I was glad I was on my knees—already in praying position.

We waited a few minutes and then got up to check things out. We found a small pool of blood where the elk had been. After searching the area below us with his binoculars, Randy spotted the bull. He quietly studied the wound through the lenses and determined by the bull's behavior that my shot was a fatal hit. However, he suggested we wait two hours before moving toward the downed elk to allow it time to expire.

Finally, though it was dark, we started searching with flashlights. We quickly discovered the tough old bull still had some life in him. He jumped up and stumbled through the blackness of the forest, leaving Randy to make the only decision that made good sense. We would head back to camp and return to the scene at daylight. Thus began one of the longest nights of my life.

It would be hard to number how many times I retook the shot that night as I ate supper, washed up, and prayed. With my head on my pillow, I watched over and over and over as my arrow took off and flew between the tree trunks. I heard the thud of its impact on the elk and heard Eddy repeat, "It wasn't a pass through." I was worried.

I think I drifted off to sleep around two o'clock, and the alarm sounded at four. Though I'd only slept a couple of hours, I catapulted off my cot like a jet off the deck of an aircraft carrier. I couldn't wait to get back to tracking the bull. We got to the scene of the shot, and I'm happy to report that after 20 minutes or so of searching, I heard Randy call to us from down the hill just below the flat: "Here he is!" What sweet words!

The big-bodied bull turned out to be an unusually large 5 x 5 that Randy said should be measured for a possible record-book entry in its class. I never did have it tallied, because in my estimation they don't get any bigger than they do when they come with a muscle-testing shot and a long, painful overnight wait on a quiet Montana mountain.

Steve's Shaky Arms Elk Roast

3 lbs. elk shoulder or rump roast	2 T. Worcestershire sauce
2 cups beef broth	2 tsp. thyme, dried
½ cup red wine vinegar	6 new potatoes, quartered
3 cloves garlic, crushed	1 lb. carrots, sliced
1 onion, chopped	1½ T. all-purpose flour
¼ cup mustard	½ cup water

Rinse the thoroughly thawed elk roast in cold water, removing as much blood as possible. Pat the roast dry and place in a large ziplock bag or glass bowl.

Mix the beef broth, red wine vinegar, garlic, onion, mustard, Worcestershire sauce, and thyme for the marinade. Cover the meat with the marinade and put in the refrigerator for 24 hours.

Place the elk and marinade in a Crock-Pot. Cook on high for 4½ to 5 hours or until meat is tender and done.

Remove the elk meat from the liquid and allow meat to sit for 10 minutes before slicing.

Remove 2 cups of broth and set aside for gravy.

Using the remaining broth, boil the potatoes and carrots until tender.

In a skillet on medium heat, mix the flour and water together. Add the set-aside broth and cook until the gravy is thick.

Serve and enjoy!

SOUL FOOD

Blessed is the man who trusts in the LORD and whose trust is the LORD. For he will be like a tree planted by the water, that extends its roots by a stream and will not fear when the heat comes; but its leaves will be green, and it will not be anxious in a time of drought nor cease to yield fruit (Jeremiah 17:7-8).

"Save Some for Me" Elk Stew

2 lbs. elk roast, cubed
2 T. olive oil
4 cups beef broth
2 cups potatoes, sliced or cubed
2 cups carrots, finely chopped
2 cups celery, finely chopped

1 cup mushrooms, finely chopped
1½ tsp. kosher salt
1 T. dried rosemary
3 cloves garlic, minced
½ cup red wine (or ½ cup beef broth)

Sauté elk meat in olive oil. Place the meat in a slow cooker. Add beef broth that has been brought to a boil (to reduce cooking time). Cook on high until the meat is tender, 6 to 8 hours.

When the meat is cooked, remove the lid and add vegetables, spices, and red wine. Add additional broth if necessary to cook the veggies.

Bring to a boil and then lower heat. Continue to cook until the vegetables are done, approximately 1 hour.

Return meat to the simmering pot of veggies and serve.

This dish is even better the second day when the flavors have had time to mingle more!

SOUL FOOD

Search me, O God, and know my heart; try me and know
my anxious thoughts; and see if there be any hurtful way in me,
and lead me in the everlasting way
(Psalm 139:23-24).

More Than One Bullet?

NATHAN AND I ARRIVED AT THE PETRICH FAMILY ranch mid-afternoon on the day before our first elk hunt. We enjoyed meeting our guide's young family, and then we unloaded our gear into the nice cabin we'd be using. Before we had unpacked everything, Randy was standing at the door with his vehicle keys in hand.

"You guys can finish this up later. Right now we need to go to the shooting range to make sure your rifles are shooting right."

My sense of humor couldn't pass up a response I was sure would get a chuckle from our hunting host. "But, Randy, I can't do that. I only brought one bullet."

He didn't smile like I thought he would. Instead he replied, "Are you serious?"

Even though it seemed I had totally sideswiped Randy with my attempt at levity, I couldn't help but follow to the punch line. "Well, I know we're only allowed one elk, so I figured I only needed one bullet."

"Steve, you've got to be kidding!" The mischief in his voice gave away the fact that I was the one who'd been had. Randy had probably heard every joke and quip about the woods from hunters, and I obviously wasn't the first who had tried the "I only brought one bullet" comment. It was nice of him to play along.

As it turned out, it was a very good thing I'd brought two boxes of .270 bullets. Nathan and I used half a dozen each at the shooting range until Randy felt confident our rifles were working and our shooting skills were acceptable. A few days later, I would use up another five trying to bring down my first bull.

Nathan's kill required only two rounds. He and Randy managed to crawl within 75 yards of a nice 6 x 6. Nathan's first elk fell where it was standing when the shot was taken.

The next day, around five o'clock in the evening, on the same mountain but higher up, it was my turn. We stalked to within 250 yards of another 6 x 6. I laid my rifle across a downed log and took aim. The wind was about 30 miles per hour in my face when I pulled the trigger. Randy was watching through the binoculars and saw the bullet strike the ground about ten yards below the bull. The beast didn't even flinch. The wind was so strong and making so much noise, the elk seemed to have not heard the shot. He had no idea we were in the area.

"Steve, take another shot but this time aim about six to eight inches over the bull above the base of the neck."

I followed his guidance, set the crosshairs above the hairline of the base of the animal's neck, and pulled the trigger. The bull hunched and then ran straight up the hill.

Randy watched him through his binoculars and gave me a post-shot report. "You hit him, but I'm not sure it was high enough in the vitals. We'll wait about 30 minutes, and then we've gotta get up this mountain to see if we can finish him off before he goes into the dark timber."

Randy soon decided 30 minutes would take us too close to sunset, so about 15 minutes later we were sneaking up the mountain, staying just inside the pines that edged the open range where the bull had been feeding. We climbed about 1000 yards without stopping, and my Tennessee flatlander lungs felt like they were on fire. We needed to hurry.

Randy Petrich

Finally we got up on a flat and were able to crawl out to take a look at the area Randy thought the bull might have escaped to. We were a mere 200 yards from the edge of the dark timber he'd mentioned earlier. He had a worried look on his face as he glassed the hillside. Suddenly and thankfully he whispered, "There he is!"

Randy quickly removed his pack and asked for mine to make a shooting rest for me to use. "Hurry! Lie down and see if you can find the bull in your scope. The window of light we need to close the deal on this bull is closing fast."

With my nerves messing with my head—and thus my eyesight—it wasn't easy to peer through the eyepiece of my scope and search the mountainside for the elk. Randy watched my barrel and kept redirecting it like a gunner's mate corrects a cannon on a battleship. Then I uttered the words he wanted to hear: "Got 'im!"

I flipped the safety off on my rifle, held steady, and fired. The light was now low enough I could see the fire leave the end of the rifle barrel. The elk stooped again and then trotted closer to the large timber.

"Shoot again, Steve!" Randy commanded.

I sent round four into the elk that was now moving slowly. Round five followed. They both connected.

Feeling quite sure the elk wouldn't get far into the dark timber, Randy said, "Let's go get your bull!" Sure enough, the brute had gone only about ten yards into the deep stand of pines before he expired. How glad I was that I had only been joking about bringing just one bullet. And that gave me some spiritual insight too.

Now I know why young David picked up five stones instead of just one when he was preparing to face Goliath. He figured he needed some back-up ammo, which tells me he was more than a harp player, songwriter, and warrior. He was also a good hunter. And the fact that he still had four "bullets" left in his clip after slaying Goliath tells me he was a better shot than I am. (But I wonder if he had a 30-mile wind in his face when he slung his first round at the giant.)

Elk Crock-Pot Super Supper

2 lbs. elk roast, cut into 3-inch cubes
4 large potatoes, cut into chunks
4 carrots, sliced on the diagonal
3 stalks of celery, chopped
salt
pepper

1 10.5-oz. can cream of mushroom
  soup
1 soup can of water
1 envelope dry onion soup mix
2 tsp. garlic powder

Place meat on the bottom of the Crock-Pot. Add vegetables on top. Salt and pepper to taste.

Mix together the remaining ingredients and pour over the meat and veggies. Cook on low heat for 6 to 8 hours.

SOUL FOOD

Gideon went in and prepared a young goat and unleavened bread from an ephah of flour; he put the meat in a basket and the broth in a pot, and brought them out to him under the oak and presented them (Judges 6:19).

Sweet and Sour Elk Meatballs

1 lb. ground elk meat
1 tsp. salt
½ tsp. pepper

½ cup bread crumbs
1 egg, slightly beaten
3 T. olive oil

Sweet and Sour Sauce

¾ cup ketchup
⅛ cup apple cider vinegar

⅛ cup soy sauce
¼ cup brown sugar

Mix meat, salt, pepper, bread crumbs, and egg in a medium bowl. Form into balls and brown in hot oil. Remove the meatballs from the oil and place on paper towels to drain.

Combine the ketchup, apple cider vinegar, soy sauce, and brown sugar, mixing thoroughly.

Return the meatballs to the skillet and pour the sweet-and-sour sauce over them. Simmer for 30 minutes until the meatballs are thoroughly cooked. (Add additional water if necessary.)

Tender Elk Roast

4 to 5 lbs. elk roast	1 T. garlic salt
1 quart water	1 T. onion salt
1 cup vinegar	1 T. Worcestershire sauce
3 T. salt	1 large onion, sliced
1 T. pepper	1 can cream of mushroom soup

Place the roast in a large bowl.

Mix the next 7 ingredients and pour over uncooked elk roast. Cover and marinate overnight.

Pour off juice and set aside. Place meat in a covered roasting pan. Add the juice from the marinade along with enough water so the liquid is halfway up the meat. Add the onion.

Roast for 2 hours at 350°.

Remove the meat and slice into ¼-inch thick slices. Put back into the roaster. Pour mushroom soup over the top and stir into the broth.

Bake at 300° for 2½ hours.

Tip: Serve with Sweet, Sweet Potato Casserole (page 218).

SOUL FOOD

Praise the LORD from the earth, sea monsters and all deeps; fire and hail, snow and clouds; stormy wind, fulfilling His word; mountains and all hills; fruit trees and all cedars; beasts and all cattle; creeping things and winged fowl (Psalm 148:7-10).

Zach's Slow-cooked Elk Pepper Steak

submitted by Dena Petrich

2 lbs. elk round steak
2 T. cooking oil
¼ cup soy sauce
1 cup onion, chopped
1 garlic clove, minced
1 tsp. sugar
½ tsp. salt
¼ tsp. pepper

¼ tsp. ground ginger
4 tomatoes, cut into eighths (or
  16-oz. can of tomatoes with liquid,
  cut up)
2 large green peppers, cut into strips
½ cup cold water
1 T. cornstarch
noodles or rice

Cut steak into strips. Put oil into skillet and heat. Add steak and brown, and then transfer meat to a slow cooker.

Combine the soy sauce, onion, garlic, sugar, salt, pepper, and ground ginger. Sprinkle over elk.

Cover and cook on low for 5 to 6 hours or until meat is tender.

Add tomatoes and green peppers, and continue to cook on low for 1 hour.

Combine the cold water and cornstarch to make a paste. Stir into slow cooker liquid. Cook on high until liquid is thick.

Prepare noodles or rice per package instructions.

Serve steak mixture over the noodles or rice.

SOUL FOOD

When a man's ways are pleasing to the LORD, He makes even his enemies to be at peace with him. Better is a little with righteousness than great income with injustice (Proverbs 16:7-8).

The Petrichs

THROUGH THE YEARS OF WRITING BOOKS FOR HUNTERS, I've mentioned more than once my adventures with hunting guide Randy Petrich of Rising Son Outfitters. Without exception, my hunts with Randy have been incredible and exciting. From the first trip in 1996 with my son, Nathan, to hunt the mighty elk to more recent spring season bear hunts, I have great memories.

One thing I so enjoy about my time with Randy is getting to see such a close-knit family. Randy and his wife have three boys: Zach, Zane, and Zander. Recently their proud dad and mom sent picture proof that in the Petrich DNA is a hunting gene that is passed on to their offspring.

Another very enjoyable part of hunting with "Rising Son Outfitters" is eating the meals Randy's wife, Dena, makes out of Montana elk. It's the kind of eating that would tempt a visiting Easterner to make a call back home to say, "Pack up all our belongings, rent a U-Haul for the furniture, throw everything else into the truck, and come on out here to Montana! We're moving in with the Petrichs!"

Of course, I'm not recommending that anyone do such a thing, but it has crossed my mind. Instead of having all of us move in with such a fine family and emptying their freezer, Dena has graciously provided two favorite recipes you can use to create your own delicious meals.

And when you prepare your versions of these dishes and offer grace, why not include the Petrichs? Folks like them deserve to be blessed!

Zach Petrich

Zane and Randy Petrich

83

Zane's Elk Round Steak 'n' Gravy

submitted by Dena Petrich

2 lbs. elk round steak
1 cup flour
2 T. cooking oil
1 envelope dry onion soup mix

1 10.5-oz. can cream of chicken
  soup
2 soup cans of water

Preheat oven to 350°.

Cut steak into strips and dredge in flour. Heat oil in skillet and add steak. After browning steak, transfer to an oven-safe roaster.

Sprinkle dry onion soup mix on steak. Add cream of chicken soup and spread over meat. Add enough water to cover the meat.

Bake at 350° for 3 hours.

Tip: Serve with Mashed Potatoes (page 215).

Elk Burger Soup

2 lbs. ground elk meat
  (or any wild game meat)
3 T. cooking oil
1 cup onions, chopped
1 cup potatoes, diced
1 cup carrots, diced
1 cup cabbage, shredded
1 15-oz. can stewed tomatoes

½ cup wild rice, cooked
1 small bay leaf
½ tsp. thyme
1 tsp. black pepper
2 tsp. salt
2 cups beef broth
2 T. cider vinegar
1 quart water

Brown the ground elk in a skillet with hot oil, and then put meat into a large stew pot (or Crock-Pot). Add the rest of the ingredients.

Bring mixture to a boil and then reduce heat. Cover and simmer for 1½ hours (using a Crock-Pot increases cooking time). Add additional water as needed to keep meat moist.

Tip: Serve with Cornbread (page 222).

Santa Fe Elk Stew

This is Steve's all-time favorite use of elk or venison burger. If I'm going to be gone for several days, he usually begs me to make a pot of this stew and a tub of Coleslaw Salad to tide him over until I get back.

3 lbs. ground elk (or venison)	2 11-oz. cans of corn, drained
2 large onions, chopped	1 28-oz. can of stewed tomatoes
1 green pepper, chopped	2 cups water
1 red pepper, chopped	1 10-oz. can Rotel tomatoes (diced
2 cups mushrooms, sliced	tomatoes and green chilies)
¼ cup vegetable oil	2 packets dry taco mix
1 15.5-oz. can of kidney beans,	1 packet dry ranch dressing mix
drained	2 T. chili powder
1 15-oz. can black beans, drained	salt
1 15-oz. can of pinto beans, drained	pepper

Sauté the ground meat, onions, peppers, and mushrooms in the vegetable oil until the meat is no longer pink. Drain off excess oil. Add the remaining ingredients and simmer in a Crock-Pot for 3 hours or until ready to eat. The longer it simmers, the better the flavor.

Tip: Serve with Coleslaw Salad (page 209).

SOUL FOOD

[Jesus said,] "Truly, truly, I say to you, you seek Me, not because you saw signs, but because you ate of the loaves and were filled. Do not work for the food which perishes, but for the food which endures to eternal life, which the Son of Man will give to you, for on Him the Father, God, has set His seal"
(John 6:26-27).

MOOSE

Baked Western Moose Meatballs

2 lbs. moose burger	2 cups bread crumbs
¼ tsp. garlic powder	1 tsp. salt
2 T. butter	½ tsp. cayenne
2 eggs, beaten	1 tsp. black pepper
1 cup milk	

Sauce

1 T. butter	¼ cup brown sugar
¾ cup onion, chopped	$2/3$ cup white vinegar
1 cup ketchup	2 tsp. dry mustard
1 oxo cube (or beef bouillon cube)	½ tsp. salt
dissolved in 1 cup boiling water	1 T. cornstarch
½ cup molasses	

Combine first 9 ingredients (all except sauce ingredients), and roll into 1½-inch balls. Place on a cookie sheet.

Bake at 350° for 20 minutes or until cooked through. Transfer meatballs from the cookie sheet to a casserole dish or small roaster.

Combine sauce ingredients in a pot and boil until thick. Pour sauce over meatballs.

Bake at 325° for 1 hour.

Moose with Sour Cream

¼ cup flour
½ tsp. salt
½ tsp. pepper
1 tsp. garlic powder
1 lb. round moose steak,
   cut into narrow strips
2 T. cooking oil

¾ cup onion, chopped
1 cup beef broth
½ tsp. thyme
1 10- or 12-oz. can sliced mushrooms
¾ cup peas, frozen
½ cup sour cream
12 oz. rice

Combine flour, salt, pepper, and garlic powder.

Dredge meat strips in flour mixture.

Heat oil in a deep frying pan. Brown the meat. Add onions, broth, thyme, and the liquid only from the mushrooms. Cover and simmer for 45 minutes or until meat is tender.

Add mushrooms, peas, and sour cream, mixing thoroughly.

Cook over medium heat for 5 to 7 minutes.

Prepare rice according to package instructions.

Serve moose on a bed of steamed rice.

Moose Stroganoff

1 lb. moose round steaks	10.5 oz. milk
1 cup flour	1 15-oz. can beef consommé
salt	8 oz. mushrooms, sliced
pepper	3 T. butter
¼ cup olive oil	½ cup red wine (or beef broth)
1 cup onion, diced	1 8-oz. pkg. noodles
1 cup celery, thinly cut	Parmesan cheese as desired
1 10.5-oz. can cream of mushroom soup (or cream of chicken soup)	garlic powder as desired

Beat steaks with a meat mallet to tenderize and flatten.

Mix flour, salt, and pepper. Dredge the meat in this mixture and then cut into bite-sized pieces.

Heat olive oil in a skillet, add steaks, and brown. Remove steaks from skillet and place in a bowl. (Do not drain the oil from the skillet.)

Put onion and celery in the skillet and cook until almost dry, stirring frequently. Place browned meat back into the skillet to warm.

Pour cream of mushroom soup into frying pan and add milk. Add beef consommé and stir.

Simmer for 5 to 7 minutes, making sure mixture comes to a boil.

In a separate pan, sauté mushrooms in butter and red wine.

Prepare noodles according to package instructions and drain.

Serve by placing noodles on plates, adding a little butter or margarine, and then covering with the hot moose mixture. Top with mushrooms and dust with Parmesan cheese and garlic.

SOUL FOOD

How blessed is everyone who fears the LORD, who walks in His ways. When you shall eat of the fruit of your hands, you will be happy and it will be well with you. Your wife shall be like a fruitful vine within your house, your children like olive plants around your table
(Psalm 128:1-3).

CARIBOU

Kenneth's Caribou

I'VE RECEIVED A LOT OF PICTURES IN MY MAILBOX and inbox from hunters who want to share their experiences. I totally enjoy each one. I like to imagine what is being said when the photos are taken because of two things I'm sure are true: 1) the animal that was taken in the picture is probably still warm, and 2) the hunter and his photographer are still basking in the glow of the success they're capturing via their cameras. While all the photos bring a smile to my face, there's one picture I received of a man and his downed animal that gave me as much joy as all the others combined. It featured the face of the one who introduced me to hunting way back around 1963. His name is Kenneth Bledsoe.

In my book *A Look at Life from a Deer Stand,* I shared about Kenneth inviting me to go on a squirrel hunt on an October day in West Virginia. On that morning, my future as an outdoorsman was set in place. I'll be forever grateful for his willingness to take a young, city-slicker kid into the woods to help me discover that I was born to be a hunter. Even more important, I have Kenneth to thank for guiding me to an interest that has led to many opportunities to share spiritual "trophies of truth" I've found while engaged in hunting.

Squirrels, rabbits, deer, and grouse were plentiful on the hillsides around Kenneth's house, so he was quite content to hunt close to home. Every once in a while he would venture to a different county in West Virginia to hunt with family or friends, but mostly his exploits were confined to Mason County. However, in his heart there was a quiet longing that was finally met. The story is best told in his own words:

> I always dreamed of going to a place to hunt and fish where I couldn't hear any planes, trains, chainsaws, cars, and tractor trailers. A place where I couldn't see anybody other than the hunter I was with. Then one day the Lord blessed me and made my dream come true. I got to go hunt the mighty Canadian caribou!
>
> I drove with my friend Maurice Pendleton from my house in West Virginia to Raddison, Quebec, on the edge of

the Hudson Bay. We couldn't go any further by car, so we boarded a bush plane and flew 300 miles into the wilderness. We were 1,585 miles from my front porch! With only the sound of birds and the sight of lakes and beautiful rock formations everywhere, we camped, hunted, and fished for almost a week. It could not have been a better trip. And best of all, we both filled our caribou tags and took home some of the best meat we'll ever enjoy. May God be praised for His marvelous gifts!

As far as I'm concerned, no one deserved the trip more than Kenneth. God has some great people on the planet, and Ken's one of them in my record book! An even more enjoyable part of this story is how Kenneth's wife never wasted an ounce of her hubby's hard-earned and hard-hunted critters. Whether it was fresh rabbit, squirrel, or the season's first deer, Evelyn's skill at the skillet was amazing...and still is. Her culinary treatment of the caribou Kenneth brought home honored the effort he'd made to get it. Thankfully, she was willing to share her recipe!

Steve with Kenneth Bledsoe

Evelyn's Stew of Caribou

1 lb. lean caribou, chopped into
2-inch cubes
1 quart beef stock
2 medium potatoes, peeled and
diced
4 large carrots, peeled and cut into
large chunks
3 stalks celery, cut into large chunks
2 large onions, quartered
3 large tomatoes, quartered

3 garlic cloves, finely minced
1 bay leaf
1½ cups red wine (or beef stock)
½ cup all-purpose flour
1 stick butter, melted
2 T. thyme leaves, finely chopped
1 tsp. rosemary leaves, fresh, finely
chopped
salt
pepper

Place caribou meat in a large, heavy pot. Cover with beef stock and cook on low for 45 minutes.

Add potatoes, carrots, celery, onions, tomatoes, garlic, bay leaf, wine. (Add additional beef stock if needed to keep meat covered.) Cook until vegetables are tender, approximately 20 minutes.

In a separate bowl, mix the flour and melted butter. Add to stew (for thickening). Add rosemary, thyme, salt to taste, and pepper to taste. Continue to simmer for 25 minutes, allowing the flavors to mix.

SOUL FOOD

Behold, I [Jesus] stand at the door and knock;
if anyone hears My voice and opens the door, I will come in
to him, and will dine with him, and he with Me
(Revelation 3:20).

Kenneth's Caribou Chops

Marinade

¼ cup olive oil

1 T. Worcestershire sauce
1 T. garlic, minced

Caribou Chops

1 lb. caribou steaks, cut ½-inch thick
1/8 cup vegetable oil
1 medium onion, sliced

1 cup mushrooms, sliced
1 tsp. steak seasoning
1 tsp. black pepper

Combine marinade ingredients and pour into bowl. Add steak and marinate for 24 hours.

Remove meat and pat dry.

Heat the oil in a heavy skillet on medium-high heat. Cook the steaks for 3 minutes on each side. Add onions and mushrooms, placing the steaks on top of the onions so the meat is away from direct heat. Sprinkle the steak with the seasonings. Cook until the steak and vegetables are done to your liking.

ANTELOPE

Where the Antelope Play

OF ALL THE ANIMALS I'VE PURSUED in my long and enjoyable life as a hunter, the antelope is one I've yet to take. However, I've been there when one went down. Nathan, my son, and I went to Wyoming to hunt mule deer with a gentleman we met at one of our concerts. The ranch was a mere 20,000 acres, hardly enough room to turn our truck around, but we managed to have a great time. We scored on a couple of nice 4 x 4s with bodies the size of our Tennessee cows.

We were grateful for the experience and filled our deer tags early in our hunt. Since we had a couple days left to enjoy the territory, we were delighted when we learned that our host had some hunting of his own to do because he'd secured four antelope doe tags. We were privileged to go along with him.

While driving around the ranch, we topped a tall hill and came to a sudden stop. Mr. Z grunted the word "antelope," threw his door open, told us to sit still, and hurriedly grabbed his .308 Weatherby from behind the seat. He slowly walked around the back of the vehicle and appeared again at the passenger side. He walked by us and then stepped carefully to the hood of the truck and laid his rifle across it.

We looked hard for the antelope he'd seen and nearly didn't find them. To us they were little white specks in the distance. Mr. Z had a different view through his powerful scope. I watched him hone in on a target and draw a deep breath.

Nathan coughed a little bit but very quietly.

Mr. Z lifted his eye from the scope. "Boys, keep 'er quiet in there, if you will."

Nathan and I were afraid to turn our heads to look at each other, but we did. We couldn't believe that one little subdued cough might affect the crosshairs that were placed on the target we figured had to be at least 500 yards away. We'd heard of people taking 500-yard shots, but we'd never seen anyone attempt a shot that long. We held our breaths while we waited for the blast of the rifle.

Finally the trigger was pulled. I thought I saw one white speck suddenly disappear, but I struggled to believe it.

Mr. Z jacked another shell into the chamber and laid his gun across the hood again. This time it was to make sure the antelope was still down. After studying the scene for a minute, he unloaded the Weatherby, recased it, put it in the back, hopped behind the wheel, and we drove to the downed antelope.

The chance to get our first mulies was exciting enough, but we never expected to get to witness a man who was so connected to his weapon. It was inspiring! Every time I go to a range now to fire my guns, I think of Mr. Z.

Antelope Supreme

2 lbs. antelope steak, cut into ½-inch cubes
3 T. olive oil
1 large onion, diced
1 cup mushrooms, sliced
1 medium green pepper, diced
1 tsp. black pepper

1 tsp. kosher salt
1 tsp. garlic powder
1 28-oz. can stewed tomatoes
1 cup beef broth
1 T. paprika
1 T. marjoram
3 cups egg noodles, cooked

In a skillet with olive oil, brown the antelope meat. Add the onion, mushrooms, and green pepper. Stir-fry for 5 minutes or so.

In a large, heavy pot, combine the meat mixture with the remaining ingredients.

Cover and simmer for 45 minutes. Approximately 20 minutes into the simmering, prepare the noodles according to package directions and drain.

Add the noodles to the meat mixture, and continue to simmer for 10 to 15 minutes. Add additional broth or water if desired.

SOUL FOOD
Your word I have treasured in my heart, that I may not sin against You (Psalm 119:11).

Antelope and Noodle Skillet Meal

2 lbs. ground antelope	1 lb. noodles
1 medium onion, chopped	1 tsp. sugar
2 T. cooking oil	1 lb. Velveeta cheese, cubed
1 quart tomato juice	salt
2 cups water	pepper

In a large skillet, brown the antelope and onion in oil. Drain off as much grease as possible. Add the tomato juice and water and bring to a boil.

Add the noodles and cook until they are tender.

Turn off the heat and add the Velveeta. Cover and let sit until the cheese is fully melted.

Tip: Serve with Green and White Salad (page 209).

SOUL FOOD

*"If your enemy is hungry, feed him, and if he is thirsty,
give him a drink; for in so doing you will heap burning coals
on his head." Do not be overcome by evil, but overcome
evil with good* (Romans 12:20-21).

BEAR

Ready, Aim, Load

MY MAIDEN VOYAGE INTO THE WILD in search of bear could not have taken place in a more beautiful part of the planet—Montana. Eddy Richey and I joined guide Randy Petrich for a springtime trip into the mountains near Livingston. The adventure yielded one of the most unforgettable moments I've ever had…and one of the most embarrassing.

Eddy scored early in the week with a nice cinnamon-colored black bear. Though his success was ultra exciting, our ascent behind Randy as we hurried up a mountainside to get into position for the shot nearly caused our Eastern, out-of-shape lungs to explode. With the dreaded anticipation of having to make another challenging climb for my chance at a shot looming over us, the news that we'd be riding horses to another area was a huge relief.

With one bear already on the hook, we took off before daylight the next day. We rode a couple of hours into the high country. Around mid-morning, we quietly (well, as quietly as three people mounted on horses can be) slipped through some tall pines on the way up to a point where we could set up and glass distant meadows for browsing bears. Just before we exited the thick stand of pines to cross a sizable meadow, I looked ahead and saw something unusual in the middle of the field.

"Randy!" I whispered. "Randy, stop! What is that spot in the field? Is that a panther?"

Randy pulled his binoculars up to his eyes. "Nope," he replied. "No such thing in these parts. We have mountain lions or cougars, but that darkness is the top of a black bear. He's down in a ditch. Let's dismount and stay back here in the shadows of these pines. We'll wait for him to show more of himself."

Randy had hardly finished his instructions when the bear walked out of the ditch and looked right toward us. In that same instant, one of the horses decided it was time to relieve himself on the hard ground of the trail. It sounded like water from a garden hose hitting concrete. I stared at the horse and almost groaned. Randy quickly settled my fear that the bear might get nervous and take off. "It's okay, Steve. Bears can't see all that well. He probably hears the splashing, but with us being back in these shadows, I don't think he's figured out what we are. Plus the wind is blowing toward us, which is in our favor."

Then came the announcement I'd been waiting for. Without having to take another look at the bear with his binoculars, Randy said, "Steve, that bear's a big boar! He's by himself, and he's a shooter! If you want him, you'd better hurry up and get ready. He's not going to stand there very long."

Randy didn't have to say anything more. As fast as I could move, I slipped my .270 out of the saddle-mounted scabbard. I slowly approached a big, trunked pine that was about two yards in front of us. I leaned up against it for shot stability. The bear was just standing there broadside, about 75 yards out, his face turned toward me. I placed the crosshairs on his vitals. I slid the safety off, slowly pressed the trigger, and waited for the explosion to surprise me. But what I heard when the trigger mechanism dropped was bewildering and embarrassing. "Click!" If someone had been doing live commentary on the shot, it would have gone like this: "He's ready! He's aiming! Oh oh. Now he's loading!"

In the quiet of the woods, the click sounded like a .22 rifle shot. I couldn't believe it. In the excitement of the moment, I'd forgotten the most important component of the deal closer—having bullets in the gun. My rifle wasn't loaded because I'd been following Randy's safety policy (good for man and horse) of not chambering a bullet until the opportunity for a shot was presented.

Eddy was filming the entire debacle, and I knew Randy was watching me. I kept my eye on the bear and slowly felt for the bolt of the rifle. I'm not sure, but I think I heard some snickering coming from the peanut gallery. Perhaps it was coming from the horses... The bear continued to stare in our direction, still standing broadside, as if waiting for me to get my act together.

It's hard to subdue the sound of metal sliding against metal, but I managed to get a round into the chamber without spooking the beast. With the gun now loaded, I checked the safety once more. I lowered my eye to the scope rim and aimed. When I pulled the trigger this time, I felt the jolt of the shot against my shoulder. I watched through the scope as the bear fell right where it had been standing. The deal was done. All that was left to do was put up with the anticipated thousand or two comments about my goof from the two onlookers. And even more distressing was that I knew the moment was captured on film.

Randy later commented on how composed I seemed in the face of the blunder. He was being a nice man. So how do I feel about my "ready, aim, load" moment today? While it wasn't one of my more stellar performances as a hunter, I'm grateful for the outcome. (I'm sure the bear regretted it though.) As I often do, I looked for a good lesson to take away from the experience. I did find one that I kept repeating to Randy and Eddy each time they poked me with their fun stick. You're welcome to use it too when you need it: "Greatness is not found in perfection; it's found in recovery."

Country-style Bear Steaks

Warning: Approximately 5 percent of black bears carry trichinella spiralis, a parasite known to cause trichinosis. To avoid this health hazard, be sure the meat is cooked and handled properly. The safest way to eat bear meat is to make sure it is cooked until it falls off the bone, until it is fork tender.

bear steaks	1½ cups flour
marinade (see Gravies, Marinades, & Sauces, page 239)	½ cup cooking oil
1 tsp. salt	1 pkg. dry onion soup mix (or ½ cup chopped onion)
½ tsp. pepper	Water
1 tsp. garlic powder (or 3 garlic cloves, crushed)	

Marinate the bear steaks in your favorite marinade.

Remove the meat and rinse with cold water. Pat dry.

Slice the steaks into desired portions, approximately ¼-inch thick. Using a tenderizing meat mallet, pound the meat until tender.

Add the salt, pepper, and garlic powder to 1 cup of flour. Dredge the steaks in the flour mixture.

Heat the oil on medium-high in a skillet with a lid. Brown the bear meat for 2 to 3 minutes on each side. Add the dry onion soup mix and enough water to cover meat. Cover tightly and simmer until meat is tender, approximately 1 hour.

Uncover and gradually add additional flour until the liquid in the skillet thickens to a nice gravy consistency.

Tip: The tenderness of bear meat depends on the age of the bear. When preparing meat from a young bear, marinating isn't necessary, although it will tenderize and help remove any gamy taste. Meat from older bears should always be marinated before cooking. Bear meat is great in casseroles and stews too.

Bear Stew

Warning: To avoid parasites, it is imperative that bear meat is cooked and handled properly. The safest way to eat bear meat is to make sure it is cooked until it falls off the bone, until it is fork tender.

Meat Preparation

bear meat, cut into 1-inch squares
1 cup flour

½ cup cooking oil

Stew Preparation

onions, carrots, potatoes, tomatoes,
   other veggies as desired
1 quart beef broth

2 to 4 T. flour
2 T. parsley, dry
1 tsp. sage, dry

Meat Preparation

Like all wild game, the gamy taste of bear meat is from the fat and connecting tissue. Here's a great way to prepare bear.

Cut the meat into 1-inch squares, roll in flour, and fry in hot oil until brown on the outside.

Place the bear meat in a large pot and cook (boil, bake, or Crock-Pot) until it is tender and falling apart.

Put the bear meat in the refrigerator and let cool until the next day.

Take the meat out and scrape away the fat.

Stew Preparation

In a large pot, boil the vegetables in the beef broth on medium heat for 15 to 20 minutes. If you're including tomatoes, add them during the last 5 minutes of the cooking time.

Add the bear meat, and let the meat and vegetables simmer together for 45 minutes.

Add flour to thicken the broth to make gravy. Start with 2 tablespoons of flour and add more until desired consistency is attained.

Add the parsley and sage. Simmer 5 more minutes and serve.

Black Bear Bologna

Warning: To avoid parasites, it is imperative that bear meat is cooked and handled properly. The safest way to eat bear meat is to make sure it is cooked until it falls off the bone, until it is fork tender.

4 lbs. ground bear meat	3 tsp. sugar
¼ cup Morton's Tender Quick Meat Cure	1 T. lemon pepper
	½ T. black pepper, freshly ground

Mix all ingredients well and refrigerate overnight in a ziplock bag.

The next day form the meat mixture into 1-pound rolls.

Using a cold smoker, smoke meat for 3 hours. Finish by cooking the meat on a gas grill for 45 minutes or so. Be careful to not overcook, but make sure the meat is done inside.

Cool, slice, and eat.

Tip: Although bear meat is best for this recipe, caribou, deer, and snow goose also work.

Joe's Big Bear

as told by Joe Emmert

I SHOT MY 350-POUND BLACK BEAR IN SEPTEMBER OF 2006 near Red Lake, Ontario, Canada. It was on the first day of a one-week hunting and fishing trip. To get there, we drove about five hours north of International Falls, Minnesota. That's where all roads north in that area end. On the first afternoon of our hunt, I'd only been in my treestand around five minutes. I barely got settled down when I saw motion through the trees. It was black and materialized into a bear—a big one!

The bear slowly came into range. I fired one round from my rifle. The big black bulldozer took off! I lowered my gun and quickly climbed down from the stand. I reloaded and followed the freshly made path of the bear through the thick underbrush. Believe me, since I didn't see the bear fall, my heart was pounding its way up my throat as I looked for him. And, yes, my finger was poised on the safety, ready to click it off and shoot if I had to. Finally I saw it. As I approached the mountain of black fur, my imagination threatened, trying to make me believe the bear was still breathing. But it wasn't.

I tried to call my hunting partners on my walkie-talkie but was out of range. To get a little more height for the antenna, I went back to my treestand. I reached base camp and asked for help.

When the needed help finally arrived, we headed to my bear. It was all the four of us could do to get that big fella into the boat to go back to camp!

Since I'd taken the bear on the first day of the trip, I had nothing to do but watch the eagles, fish for walleye, and enjoy the sunsets over Red Lake for the rest of the week. It was a hard job, but someone had to do it.

Thanks to plenty of good coolers and lots of dry ice, we made a legal immigrant of that bear. My family enjoyed the meat for quite a while. I continue to enjoy the bear rug on the wall, but the best part of the experience is telling the story to my grandchildren—with some grandfatherly exaggerations for the sake of drama thrown in, of course.

Joe's Big Bear Roast

Warning: To avoid parasites, it is imperative that bear meat is cooked and handled properly. The safest way to eat bear meat is to make sure it is cooked until it falls off the bone, until it is fork tender.

2 to 4 lbs. of bear roast	½ tsp. black pepper
2 cups water with 1 tsp. salt	½ tsp. celery seed
1 quart tomato juice	1 medium onion, diced
¾ cup brown sugar	(Georgia Vidalia is best)
2 T. Worcestershire sauce	

Boil the bear roast in the saltwater, and then let the meat simmer for 30 minutes. Drain the fat and water. Wash away any fat or grease residue.

Place the bear meat in a Crock-Pot. Cook on high heat for 2 hours or low heat for 4 hours. Drain off visible fat.

Add the rest of the ingredients to the Crock-Pot and simmer for at least 4 hours.

Tip: Make Poor Man's Gravy (page 241) using some of the liquid in the Crock-Pot. Serve with Mashed Potatoes (page 215) and Broccoli Cauliflower Salad (page 210).

SOUL FOOD
The counsel of the LORD stands forever, the plans of His heart from generation to generation. Blessed is the nation whose God is the LORD, the people whom He has chosen for His own inheritance (Psalm 33:11-12).

Bear Breakfast Sausage

Warning: To avoid parasites, it is imperative that bear meat is cooked and handled properly. The safest way to eat bear meat is to make sure it is cooked until it falls off the bone, until it is fork tender.

bear meat	2 T. poultry seasoning (per quart
1 pork chop (per 2 pounds of bear	of meat)
meat)	1 tsp. salt
	1 tsp. pepper

Optional
1 T. Cajun spices (instead of salt and pepper)

Grind the bear meat without seasoning. Add a deboned pork chop for each 2 pounds of bear meat.

Grind the meat again, this time mixing in poultry seasoning, salt, and pepper. If preferred, Cajun spices can be used instead of salt and pepper.

Divide the prepared sausage into 1-pound packages that can be frozen until used.

Preparing Bear Breakfast Sausage

1 lb. bear breakfast sausage	½ cup green peppers, diced
3 T. cooking oil	4 flour tortillas

In a skillet with oil, brown the bear breakfast sausage. Add green peppers and mix.

Spoon mixture into a tortilla and roll up like a burrito.

Tip: The bear is a member of the pork family, so be sure the meat is thoroughly cooked—at least to 170° throughout to kill any parasites. Or make sure the meat is stored at -10° for at least 30 days.

BISON (Buffalo)

I'll never forget the look on Annie's face when she took her first bite of buffalo burger. We were at a wild game dinner where I was the keynote speaker. My "deer" wife became an instant fan of the mighty buffalo. From that meal on, she's had a bison bent. However, we discovered an issue we didn't expect. When it comes to bison, the cost per pound can rival the full weight of the animal! Knowing this makes us extra grateful for our generous buffalo-hunting friends who love to share.

Simple and Tasty Bison Burgers

1 lb. ground bison
1½ tsp. kosher salt
½ tsp. black pepper

3 T. cooking oil (do not use olive oil)
1 pkg. hamburger buns

Spread the ground bison on a cookie sheet, and sprinkle salt and pepper evenly. Shape the burger into patties. Avoid overhandling the meat, which can make it less tender.

Place the patties on a large plate, cover with plastic wrap, and allow to rest in the refrigerator for at least 1 hour.

Cook on a greased grill or skillet until the internal temperature of the burger reaches 160°.

Tip: A mature buffalo bull will average 1500 to 2000 pounds. The yield of meat for cooking can easily be in the hundreds of pounds.

SOUL FOOD

The steps of a man are established by the LORD, and He delights in his way. When he falls, he will not be hurled headlong, because the LORD is the One who holds his hand. I have been young and now I am old, yet I have not seen the righteous forsaken or his descendants begging bread (Psalm 37:23-25).

Bison Country-fried Steaks

1 lb. bison steaks, cut ½-inch thick
16 oz. Coca-Cola
1 tsp. dry steak seasoning
1 tsp. coarse ground black pepper
¾ cup all-purpose flour

¼ cup canola oil
1 small onion, chopped
1 cup mushrooms, sliced
1 cup milk

Pound the bison steaks with a mallet to tenderize the meat.

Marinate the bison meat for 24 hours in Coca-Cola (or another marinade, see "Gravies, Marinades, and Sauces," page 239).

Remove the bison from the marinade and pat dry.

Combine steak seasoning and pepper with ½ cup flour. Dredge the meat in the mixture.

In a large, heavy skillet, heat the canola oil on medium-high. When oil is hot, add the bison steaks, cooking on both sides until golden brown, approximately 4 minutes per side. Set aside.

Gravy
Brown the onion and mushrooms in the skillet of drippings from frying the bison. Stir in 2 tablespoons of flour and add the milk. Stir and simmer until thick.

Tip: Serve with Mashed Potatoes (page 215) and hot Sylvie Biscuits (page 222) for a great meal.

Bison and Mushroom Pasta

4 tsp. vegetable oil	8 oz. smoked ham, cut into strips
1 tsp. chili powder	8 oz. mushrooms, sliced
4 6-oz. bison steaks	1 12-oz. pkg. linguine
3 T. butter	4 oz. heavy cream

Mix the oil and chili powder together and rub on steaks. Allow meat to rest for 30 minutes.

In a heated saucepan, sear the steaks on both sides. Lower heat and cook until desired doneness, making sure steaks are cooked all the way through. Turn the steaks often.

Melt the butter in a sauté pan. Cook the ham and mushrooms until mushrooms are limp, approximately 4 minutes.

Prepare linguine according to package instructions and add it to the ham and mushrooms. Heat thoroughly, stirring constantly. Stir in the cream and heat until hot.

To serve, place fried bison on top of pasta or serve pasta as a side dish.

SOUL FOOD

When you lie down, you will not be afraid; when you lie down, your sleep will be sweet (Proverbs 3:24).

Bison Steaks

2 lbs. bison steaks
2 T. butter
8 oz. mushrooms, sliced

2 cloves garlic, minced (or ½ cup onions, chopped)
½ cup cooking wine

In a frying pan, brown both sides of the steaks in butter. Cook until the meat is or medium rare. Remove meat from pan and set aside to rest.

Add more butter to the skillet, if necessary, and sauté mushrooms and garlic until soft and brown. Add the cooking wine and stir for 5 minutes, allowing the flavors to mingle and the liquid to be absorbed by the vegetables. (Most of the alcohol in the wine will dissipate during cooking.)

Add the steaks to the sautéd ingredients, and continue to cook until meat attains desired doneness.

Tip: Top steaks with Homemade Barbecue Sauce (page 247) or Sweet, Red Onion Marmalade (page 249).

SOUL FOOD

*A joyful heart makes a cheerful face, but when the heart
is sad, the spirit is broken...but a cheerful heart has
a continual feast* (Proverbs 15:13,15).

WILD BOAR

Tips for Cooking Wild Boar

- Wild boar meat contains much less fat than domestically raised pork. The wild boar meat will be darker and have a different consistency. If the meat is prepared properly, it will be just as tasty.

- Trim away as much fat as possible. This means you may need to add oil or butter when cooking to keep the meat from becoming too dry.

Honey-glazed Wild Boar Steaks or Chops

2 large boar steaks or 7 chops
honey
oven bag

1 pkg. seasoning or use
McCormick's Bag & Season for
pork chops

Coat wild boar steaks or chops with honey. Following the oven bag instructions, place the meat in the oven bag. Follow the seasoning package directions and then pour into oven bag.

Cook according to the directions for pork that came with the oven bag. (Usually pork steaks cook at 350° for 30 minutes or so.)

Tip: Serve with Poor Man's Gravy (page 241), vegetables, and potatoes. Instead of gravy, try dipping the meat in applesauce.

Wild Boar Chops

Marinade

1 12-oz. can beef broth
2 cups cider vinegar
2 cups water
1½ tsp. black pepper
2 tsp. salt

2 bay leaves
1 tsp. thyme, crumbled
2 cloves garlic, chopped
½ cup cranberries

Main Ingredients

7 carrots, sliced on the diagonal
2 large onions, quartered
4 stalks celery, sliced

1 12-oz. can beef broth
1/3 cup currant jelly
½ cup all-purpose flour

In a large glass bowl, combine the marinade ingredients. Add meat to the marinade, cover, and refrigerate for 36 to 48 hours. Turn the meat every few hours.

Pour the meat and marinade into a large, heavy kettle. Cover and simmer on stove for 2½ hours or until meat is almost tender. Add the vegetables and cook until done. (If you use a Crock-Pot, cook on high for 6 to 8 hours.)

Remove the meat and vegetables from broth and cover them to keep warm.

Add 12 ounces of beef broth, currant jelly, and flour to the marinade still heating on the stove. Stir until the sauce bubbles and thickens to gravy consistency.

Pour gravy over the meat and vegetables and serve.

SOUL FOOD

Honor the LORD from your wealth and from the first of all your produce; so your barns will be filled with plenty and your vats will overflow with new wine (Proverbs 3:9-10).

Wild "Boargers" and Honey-glazed Onions

If you love onions, you'll love this dish. Serve boar sausage burgers on hamburger buns, along with other fixin's, such as french fries, pickles, and ketchup.

1/3 lb. ground wild boar sausage (per person)	1 hamburger bun (per person)
	condiments as desired

Honey-glazed Onions

golf ball-sized onions, any type, cut into quarters (2 per person)	1 T. vegetable oil
1/2 cup water	1/2 tsp. salt
	2 T. honey

Boarburgers

Form 1/3-pound patties and cook on grill to desired doneness. Serve with all the fixin's for hamburgers.

Honey-glazed Onions

Cut the stems and root ends from onions, and then peel them.

Place onions in a wok or cooking pan with water and vegetable oil. Sprinkle with salt. Cover and cook until the onions are soft, approximately 5 minutes.

Remove onions from pan and place in a small bowl. Allow to cool.

Just before serving, place the bowl of onions in the microwave and reheat until the onions are steaming hot. Remove from microwave, drizzle a small amount of honey over them, and serve.

SOUL FOOD

The LORD is my light and my salvation; whom shall I fear?
The LORD is the defense of my life; whom shall I dread?
(Psalm 27:1).

12-hour Wild Boar Chops

6 wild boar chops
1 16-oz. can chicken broth
1 10.5-oz. can cream of chicken
  soup
4 medium potatoes, cut into chunks

4 carrots, diced
2 medium onions, diced
salt, pepper, and garlic powder to
  taste

Place chops in a large pan. Pour chicken broth over chops.

In a bowl, mix the cream of chicken soup per directions on the can. Pour it over the chops as well.

Add the potatoes, carrots, and onions. Stir in the spices.

Bring mixture to a slow boil.

Pour the mixture into a Crock-Pot and let simmer for a full 12 hours, checking periodically to see if more water is needed to keep meat covered. (Wild boar chops and steaks tend to be tough, but using this method makes them tender and tasty.)

SOUL FOOD

I have fought the good fight, I have finished the course,
I have kept the faith; in the future there is laid up for me the
crown of righteousness, which the Lord, the righteous Judge,
will award to me on that day; and not only to me, but also to all who
have loved His appearing (2 Timothy 4:7-8).

JAVELINA

Javelina—The Desert Ghost

AS PROFESSIONAL MUSICIANS, ANNIE AND I TRAVEL around the United States to praise God, point people to Jesus, and encourage family values. We often use our personal experiences to illustrate biblical truths and ideas. In my case, I especially enjoy drawing on my times in the woods and hunting. One of my favorites is pointing out what happens to a "love crazy" buck. He abandons his normally cautious nature during mating season. By his extreme focus on does, he unintentionally makes himself vulnerable to the hunter's gun or bow. Using that picture as a springboard, I remind people that we too can place ourselves in spiritual—and sometimes even physical—danger when we cast aside moral alertness, especially when it comes to the opposite sex. Many who have heard this story have thanked me for sharing, saying it helped them be more careful about avoiding temptations. That's a wonderful outcome.

The other response I totally like to hear is from hunters who discover I'm "one of them and love the fair chase." Many of these individuals have been kind enough to extend an invitation to hunt with them in their neck of the woods. Through the years I've said yes to several opportunities, resulting in hunts in states as diverse as Montana, Colorado, Wyoming, Nebraska, North Dakota, South Dakota, Iowa, Kansas, Wisconsin, Arizona, New Jersey, Kentucky, Indiana, Missouri, Michigan, Illinois, Ohio, Alabama, and Mississippi. And that's not even counting where I've been to fish.

All the hunts have been memorable. I believe I could recount each one in vivid detail. But space and pages are limited, so I'll limit this tale to a special hunt in Arizona. We were going after the elusive javelina, a medium-sized creature that looks like a wild pig but is actually a member of the peccary family, a group of hoofed mammals originating from South America.

After an October evening concert, a gentleman named Richard asked me if I've ever bow-hunted the javelina. When he learned I was yet to experience the exciting "spot and stalk" style of hunting he prefers for these critters, he "forced" me to agree to join him in late January for an outdoor adventure. One reason this hunt especially appealed to me was because the Tennessee deer season is closed then so I knew I'd be antsy to engage in the fair chase.

When January came around, I had a mere two-and-a-half days available to hunt. Richard and I searched hard for a "shooter" javelina, but to no avail.

When the afternoon of the last day arrived without an arrow missing from my quiver, I contemplated the likelihood I would be going home with only memories of the attempt and some Arizona dust on my boots. Richard was bewildered at the lack of legal javelina, so he suggested we check one more spot before we made the long trek to his truck empty-handed.

Hiking uphill, we finally topped a high vista overlooking a deep canyon. We sat down with our binoculars to glass the opposite hillside. Within a couple of minutes Richard broke the silence. "There they are! And it's a good-sized group."

I found them and watched as they fed along a path and slowly moved up the hill. Nearly half a mile to their location, I figured, so I thought we'd sit and wait, hoping they'd cross to our hill and get closer to where we were. Our window of opportunity was getting smaller due to the time, so I was just a tad discouraged.

"Steve…" Richard said. He paused, as if considering what to say. "Steve, do you think you could get down this canyon and up the other side before those javelina get to the top of that hill?"

I surveyed the territory. I didn't really think I could do it, but because it might be my last chance, I responded with a very tentative yes. Then I quickly stood up, put my pack on, gathered up my bow, and looked to Richard so we could head down the steep hill.

Richard stopped me. "Here's what we gotta do," he said. "To keep the commotion down and not spook those critters, I'm going to stay right here. When you get high enough on the other side that you think you can see me through your binoculars, look over every few minutes. I'll give you hand signals to direct you to the herd. The most important signal I'll give is a 'come to full draw' motion. If you see me do that, you'll know I can see the group is getting very close to you."

I agreed to the plan and took off. It took me 30 minutes or so to get to the bottom of the ravine and up the other side high enough to find Richard through the binoculars. When I found him, he waved his arms to my left indicating which direction I should go to encounter the herd. We exchanged looks a few more times, and he kept giving me the same signal.

Suddenly I smelled something akin to the foul odor that emanates from a stockyard full of cattle. Whew! I wondered if I'd gotten within nose range of a cattle ranch. I stopped to take in what most cow people call "the sweet smell of money." As I stood there taking in the pungent odor, I decided I should look through my binoculars again and find Richard. When I found him, he was frantically and repeatedly doing the "come to full draw" motion. That's when I realized that what I was smelling was the herd of javelina approaching.

I hurriedly pocketed my binoculars, knocked an arrow, and attached the release. I got it all done just in time! I looked down the path and saw a sizable javelina male walking right toward me—and he hadn't seen me yet. I came to full draw. Just as I got the kisser button on my lip, the creature stopped and looked up to discover what was blocking his trail.

Convinced that whatever was in his way wasn't supposed to be there, he got nervous and turned around to leave. As he walked away, I thought, "Texas heart shot. It's my only chance." I took aim at the javelina's rear and let my arrow fly. He keeled over deader than an Arizona rock. The deed was done. I didn't know it, but this beast was large for its kind.

I looked across the valley toward Richard, raised my bow high with my left hand, and gave him a thumbs-up signal with my right hand. He immediately made his descent and hiked to where I was. Darkness wasn't far away as he came toward me. He was winded from the hurried climb, but he was also smiling from ear to ear. We shook hands and agreed that hardly anything could be better than this good plan that came together so well and yielded such unforgettable results.

After taking a few photos and field dressing our "desert ghost," we shared the chore of carrying the weighty prize to the truck. Thankfully it was a downhill trek the entire way.

When I got back to Tennessee I had the javelina head mounted by a local taxidermist. Looking at it reminds me of one of my most satisfying hunts. Although the meat is long gone, I still remember the delicious taste!

Arizona Javelina on Rice

1 javelina leg

1 tsp. salt

½ tsp. pepper

2 10.5-oz. cans cream of mushroom
soup

potatoes, cubed

celery, diced

carrots, diced

2 cups jasmine rice

Place the javelina leg in a Crock-Pot and cook for 8 to 12 hours (if possible, overnight) in water seasoned with salt and pepper.

After meat cools, remove the bones and shred the meat. Put the javelina in a large skillet and cook over medium heat.

Pour mushroom soup on top of meat. Add vegetables and continue simmering until the veggies are tender.

Prepare jasmine rice according to package instructions.

Serve javelina on a bed of cooked rice.

SOUL FOOD

*Submit therefore to God. Resist the devil and he will flee from you.
Draw near to God and He will draw near to you.
Cleanse your hands, you sinners; and purify your hearts,
you double-minded* (James 4:7-8).

Part 2
SMALL GAME

RACCOON

An Unlikely Food Source

WHILE THERE ARE LOTS OF GAME we could include in this book, we've chosen one you might not have considered. We include this one for sentimental reasons. It was a flavor favored by N.R. Williamson, Annie's dad. His affection for this particular animal was likely a result of remembering how it met a very real need when he was growing up and food was scarce at times.

The smell of this critter baking in the oven seemed to evoke treasured memories of his earlier years when he spent nights chasing this critter with his brothers and their rambunctious hounds. Knowing his appreciation for this food source, his wife, Sylvia, graciously accommodated his occasional hankering by serving Baked 'Coon.

Baked 'Coon

1 raccoon	1 T. rubbed sage
1 tsp. salt	1 T. Worcestershire sauce
½ tsp. black pepper	3 sticks butter
½ tsp. red pepper	10 medium sweet potatoes, baked
½ cup chopped onions	2 T. sugar
½ tsp. powdered garlic	

Boil the raccoon meat in a large pot of water until very tender, 1 to 2 hours, depending on the size of animal. Remove from water and drain.

Scrape off all fat, remove scent glands (these 4 "kernels" are the size of kidney beans, look brown and waxy, and are located under the forelegs and along the small of the back).

Cut the 'coon into sections and place in a large, shallow baking pan. Dust on all sides with salt and black and red pepper. Add onion, garlic, sage, Worcestershire sauce, and 1 stick of butter.

Set potatoes firmly on top of coon meat and sprinkle with sugar. Baste liberally with remaining butter.

Broil for approximately 20 minutes or until brown.

Remove from oven, turn meat over, and broil again until that side is brown.

Serve hot.

Tip: Serve with Tomato Gravy (page 241).

SOUL FOOD

[Jesus said,] "Blessed are those who hunger and thirst for righteousness, for they shall be satisfied" (Matthew 5:6).

SQUIRREL

Small Beginnings

WHEN I WAS INTRODUCED TO HUNTING way back in the old days, there were very few deer in my part of the world. In fact, whenever someone sighted a whitetail, the phones started ringing in the valley and the news spread quickly. Because opportunities for hunting big game were so limited, we had to be content with chasing smaller critters. Thankfully they were plentiful.

While there were sufficient numbers of squirrels, not everyone regarded them as edible. Some folks considered squirrels nothing more than large rats with bushy tails. But because they were plentiful and the meat provided a money-saving supplement of food, people were willing to learn to like eating them. Even with that, for some people a stretching of their taste buds was required to sit down and eat a meal that included this delicacy.

Fortunately, my introduction to eating squirrel took place in the dining room of the wife of the man who took me hunting for the first time. Kenneth's wife, Evelyn, has mastered the art of cooking squirrel so well that Kenneth would even crack open squirrel skulls to eat the brains. (I tried them, but I never developed a taste for it.) My first supper at the Bledsoe table with squirrel on the menu was so lip-smackin' good that from then on I was a fan of the furry little critters.

I contacted Evelyn and asked her to share her story of how she came to be such an expert with small game.

Learning to Love Squirrel and the Man Who Loves to Hunt Them

by Evelyn Bledsoe

Because no one in my family hunted, and none of us had ever eaten wild meat, I didn't realize that people actually ate the animals that roamed the fields and woods. But then I married a fine young man named Kenneth. About a month after our wedding, hunting season came in. As it approached,

I learned the reality of how opening day can affect a dedicated hunter and those he loves sharing the season with.

Kenneth, his dad, his grandfather, and several of his brothers constantly talked and planned where they'd hunt the first day—what time to be in the woods, what guns to use, what ammo, what the correct clothing would be, and on and on. They also talked about how they looked forward to their hunting successes being turned into tasty meals. That last item really got my attention.

As a newlywed, I'd just started learning how to cook. I could manage familiar meals, such as pork chops, mashed potatoes, and canned veggies. And I was slowly learning the art of cooking beef and chicken. But rabbits? Squirrels? Groundhogs? Even frogs? O my, what a challenge! I knew there'd be no way to change my man's taste for all things wild, so I resolved to learn the art of cooking wild game.

One of the first lessons I learned about making a great meal of small game was "gravy is the key." My husband had grown up on his mother's "wild" gravy, and he kindly made it clear that he wanted me to learn how to make it. He was even helpful enough to stay in the kitchen as I tried, giving me tips on how his mother had done it. After each attempt, we would mutually decide what could be done differently the next time to get the desired results. We'd add more grease, sometimes more flour, or we'd try cooking it longer. This learning process went on for months.

Finally, one evening we got a batch of gravy that generated that smile every wife loves to see on her husband. When Kenneth tasted it, he said, "That's it!" I knew his proclamation meant it was as close to his mother's recipe than any we'd made so far.

A few weeks later we again ate squirrel and gravy—this time at my in-laws' house. On the way home, my darling husband said something that was even sweeter than "That's it!" He said, "The gravy we made tasted better than Mom's!" Woo hoo! I knew I had truly arrived. It was a major culinary success.

That red-letter day happened more than 55 years ago. Yes, I'm still making wild gravy for my husband—and all our kids and grandkids. And yes, they all hunt, bringing the critters in for me to cook. Even my granddaughter hunts. I've told them all that somebody in the family needs to learn to make my special gravy before I'm gone, but they don't stop eating long enough to let me teach them. They're too busy smacking their lips and diving in for seconds!

Bledsoes' Favorite Squirrel and Gravy

2 squirrels, cut into serving-size pieces (include heads if possible)	water with 4 T. salt dried red pepper flakes

Gravy

2 T. solid shortening	4½ T. flour water

The night before, put the squirrel meat in a 3-quart pan and add enough saltwater to cover. Let sit in the refrigerator overnight.

When ready to cook the squirrels, pour out the salt water. Rinse the meat with clean water.

Return the meat to the same pan, add water to cover the meat by about 3 inches. Add salt and red pepper flakes to taste. Bring to boil, and then reduce heat and let it simmer until done, about 2 hours. Watch closely. You may need to add extra water to keep the meat covered. Also, don't cook too long or the meat may fall off the bones.

When the squirrel is done, place it in a bowl and set aside. You should have 2 or 3 cups of water left in the pan to use for the gravy.

Gravy

In a large iron skillet, melt the shortening with medium heat. Add the flour a little at a time, stirring constantly. When flour is absorbed by the grease, let it brown well. Keep stirring so it doesn't burn. Add more flour or shortening to even out the ingredients and get the right gravy consistency. (Do not use milk! Milk covers the squirrel taste you want.) Taste the gravy and add salt and pepper if needed.

Let the gravy cook slowly for 25 to 30 minutes, stirring often and adding water if needed.

While the gravy is simmering, coat the squirrel meat with flour. Put the meat in another skillet with a little shortening. Brown it on both sides.

Serve the squirrel with the gravy.

Tip: Evelyn, Steve, and Annie's challenge to you: Many years ago when funds were limited, we let nothing go to waste when we ate wild game. We consumed squirrel brains, which are considered by some a delicacy. To eat squirrel brain, crack the skull with a table knife, pull the bone away, and slurp out the brain. We double-squirrel dare ya! If you take the dare, don't be surprised if you get a sudden urge to climb trees and dig for acorns.

Crock-Pot Squirrel

4 to 6 squirrels, cut into
  serving-sized pieces
¼ cup soy sauce
¼ cup of water
¼ cup brown sugar

3 T. lemon or lime juice
¼ tsp. garlic powder
¼ tsp. ground ginger
1 cup flour

Place the cut up squirrel in a Crock-Pot.

Mix rest of ingredients together and pour over the meat.

Cover and cook all day on low heat until tender.

Pour Crock-Pot contents into a skillet. Add flour and cook on top of the stove until the broth thickens into gravy.

Tip: Serve with Mashed Potatoes (page 215) and Sylvie Biscuits (page 222).

SOUL FOOD

*A lazy man does not roast his prey, but the precious
possession of a man is diligence*
(Proverbs 12:27).

Mr. Rogers' Bent Barrel

ANNIE AND I ATTENDED THE SAME JUNIOR AND SENIOR HIGH in Point Pleasant, West Virginia. Our shared past has an advantage we cherish: We enjoy remembering faces and names we both know. Among the many people we recall from time to time is the biology teacher I had in the ninth grade. His name was Mr. Jack Rogers. Although Annie didn't have the opportunity of having him for a teacher, she remembers how kind he was to all the kids outside the classroom.

Perhaps one of the reasons he was a favorite teacher was because he would often take his classes outside for a hands-on lesson in biology. Not only did our field trips make the subject more interesting, hardly anything could make a junior high kid happier than not sitting in a classroom. We knew it was going to be a great hour of school when Mr. Rogers would lead us down the hall, through a side door, and out into the sunshine. Sometimes he would herd us to a nearby patch of woods where we would look at the unique growth of ground cedar and mosses. Or he'd guide us to a small field where we would study wildflowers. On another day he might lead us to someone's front yard near the high school, with their permission, where we would huddle under an oak tree and learn about leaf structure and the power in a little acorn he picked up to show us.

On more than one occasion, as we made our way back to the school building, he would talk with us about his "other" interest—sports. He so enjoyed discussing all types of sports that it was tempting for him to spend more class time talking about them than teaching biology. In fact, knowing that Mr. Rogers was always ready to discuss sports, some students would attempt to delay learning by bringing up the subject when they first walked into class. Their hope was that his play-by-play recap would replace boring stuff, such as learning the olfactory system of the common mouse. But Mr. Rogers was much more savvy than the students, and he didn't allow that tactic to work except on a few deliberate occasions.

Mr. Rogers turned his love of football, baseball, and basketball into an opportunity to garner some local and regional fame. When he wasn't teaching or grading tests, our biology guru was writing the daily sports column for our town newspaper. Because he had a gift for turning the regular stats of a game and other sports-related stories into tall tales, his articles were rarely missed by subscribers. No local sport was left uncovered in his column, and for those of us in his classroom who preferred hunting, we were always glad to get a mention.

One of his farfetched yarns the newspaper published was penned just after squirrel season opened one year in the mid 60s. Mr. Rogers must have needed to give the story a test run to see if it worked because he told it to us first—a classroom filled with mostly gullible, nonhunting teenagers. I was in the room when it happened, but I'm glad to report that I, along with a couple of other young squirrel chasers, wasn't fooled by him. His story went something like this.

> Yep. Went squirrel huntin' over the weekend. It was good to get out there again, but there weren't a lot of bushytails in the woods. In fact, I only saw one. It came down a big red oak. I raised my shotgun to take him, and the scoundrel saw me and ran around the tree. I couldn't see him, but I could hear him squawking at me. He protested my presence for probably five minutes or more. Kinda made me mad. I figured he wasn't going to show himself again, so while he was hollerin' I took my gun and put the front part of the barrel over my knee. I pulled on it with both hands and bent that sucker into the shape of the letter "J." Then I crawled up real quiet to the backside of that oak. That squirrel was makin' so much noise, he didn't hear me coming. I figured out he was about six feet off the ground with his back toenails dug into the bark, just hanging there yappin'. I stood up and slipped that bent barrel around the right side of tree real slow and pulled the trigger. I watched that squirrel fly off to my left and land in the leaves—deader than a doornail.

When he finished the story, I saw one of my hunting buddies doing the same thing I was doing. We were checking out how many of our fellow classmates were sitting there totally believing Mr. Rogers' story and being amazed at his incredible ingenuity and strength. The funniest part to me was that after the story, Mr. Rogers went on to the day's lesson. He never broke into a mischievous grin or gave a hint that his tale was a complete fabrication.

To this day I wonder how many of the students in the classroom have grown up, gotten married, had kids, and shared that story with them. I know I've told it to my own—and just like Mr. Rogers, I let them believe every word.

Mr. Rogers' Squirrel Jambalaya

1 squirrel	1 clove garlic, minced
salt	¼ green pepper, chopped
red pepper	4 tsp. parsley, chopped
3 T. oil	1 cup rice, uncooked
2 large onions, chopped	1½ cups water
3 ribs celery, chopped	

Cut squirrel into serving pieces, sprinkle on salt and red pepper to taste while sautéing the meat in oil until brown. Remove from skillet.

Sauté onions, celery, garlic, green pepper, and parsley in the skillet until veggies are wilted.

Put squirrel back into the skillet, cover, and cook until tender.

Add rice and water and cook until the rice is done.

SOUL FOOD

The tongue of the righteous is as choice silver, the heart of the wicked is worth little. The lips of the righteous feed many, but fools die for lack of understanding (Proverbs 10:20-21).

Mr. Jack Rogers

RABBIT

IN WEST VIRGINIA WHERE I GREW UP, rabbit hunting came well after squirrel season, which usually opened in October. For that reason, by the time we were allowed to go to the fields to beat the brush in pursuit of cottontails, the weather had turned cold. Because of the frigid temperatures, rabbit hunting was ideal because we did a lot of walking instead of sitting still and waiting like we did for squirrel and deer.

In addition to a type of hunt that doesn't require stillness, we could take dogs along to find and move the rabbits for us. What luxury to have two or three good, well-trained beagle hounds to rustle rabbits out of their hiding places. Hunting without dogs was an exercise in exercise. A day without dogs meant we would have to jump up and down on brush piles and cover every inch of grassy ground to stir up the rabbits. That kind of hunting left us sweaty and exhausted from...well...acting like dogs. So it goes without saying that a good hunting beagle was worth its weight in gold.

I hunted rabbits a lot in my teen years with my mentor, Kenneth Bledsoe. I also spent a fair amount of time chasing bunnies with his young neighbor Greg Bonecutter. We made a ton of memories, but time went on and eventually responsibilities such as college, the navy, marriage, kids, and work became my focus (and rightly so). Time spent rabbit hunting declined.

About once a year, the rabbit-hunting itch was scratched when our family would drive to West Virginia to see our parents and siblings. I got to hunt with Annie's brothers. Even those chances to chase rabbits dwindled as the years went by. But whenever the opportunity presents itself, I still enjoy chasing the furry critters. And sitting around enjoying a delicious rabbit meal with family and friends is always something to look forward to.

Tips for Cooking Rabbit

- BBe Aware of the BBs. Most of us hunt rabbits with a shotgun using shells that are filled with lead or steel BBs. For that reason, it is imperative to check the meat thoroughly for the shot so that the folks who enjoy the cooked version of the critter won't have to get up from the table and make an emergency trip to a dentist. You can usually track the presence of a BB in the meat by looking closely for small, bruised slits (sometimes round) on the outside of the muscle. Some entry wounds might be filled with rabbit fur gathered by the BB on the way in. The BBs and any residual fur can be removed with a sharp, pointed knife.

- Any good chicken recipe can be used when preparing rabbit. However, because there is so little fat on the meat, you may want to use additional butter or oil when browning or basting the meat.

- Remove the scent glands. To help minimize the gamy taste of rabbit, clean out all blood and blood clots under cool running water. Remove the small scent glands (small, waxy-looking kernels under the forelegs and on both sides of the spine), being careful not to cut into them. After skinning, cut the meat into quarters. Dry the pieces and refrigerate as soon as possible. Use within three days or freeze the meat for later use.

SMALL GAME

Hasenpfeffer (a German recipe for rabbit)

1 large onion, sliced	1 large rabbit, cut into serving size
3 cups white vinegar	pieces
3 cups water	1 tsp. pepper
1 T. pickling spices	½ cup all-purpose flour
2 tsp. salt	4 or 5 slices of bacon
	2 T. butter or margarine

In a large glass bowl, combine onion, vinegar, water, and seasonings. Add rabbit pieces. Cover and refrigerate for 48 hours, turning occasionally.

Remove meat, strain the liquid, and set aside.

Dry the meat well and then coat lightly with flour. Place the rabbit and bacon strips in a heavy roasting pan.

Bake at 350° for 1 hour. Remove the rabbit and place on a warmed platter.

In a separate pan, melt the butter and gradually stir in 2 cups of the marinade. Stir in ¼ cup flour and cook until thickened. (Add more marinade if needed to reach desired consistency.)

Spoon marinade gravy over the meat and serve immediately.

Tip: Serve over roasted red potatoes that have been sprinkled with parsley.

Omie's Fried Rabbit

1 rabbit, quartered	1 tsp. salt
water with 2 T. salt	½ tsp. pepper
1 cup all-purpose flour	1 cup olive or canola cooking oil

Soak the rabbit pieces in cold saltwater and refrigerate for 1 hour. Remove the rabbit from the water and rinse with cold, clean water.

Parboil the rabbit by putting it in a pot, covering it with water, heating to a boil, and letting it boil for a few minutes. Remove the rabbit from the water and let it cool. Roll the rabbit pieces in flour seasoned with salt and pepper.

In a heavy skillet, heat the olive oil until it's hot. Fry the rabbit until it is crispy.

Rosemary Roasted Rabbit

1 rabbit, quartered
½ cup olive oil
salt
pepper

½ cup white cooking wine
2 whole garlic cloves
1 sprig dried rosemary

Coat the rabbit pieces with oil and season with salt and pepper.

Place the rabbit pieces in a roasting pan and pour the wine over it. Add garlic and rosemary and cover with foil.

Bake at 375° for 1½ hours.

SOUL FOOD

One thing I have asked from the LORD, that I shall seek: That I may dwell in the house of the LORD all the days of my life, to behold the beauty of the LORD and to meditate in His temple. For in the day of trouble He will conceal me in His tabernacle; in the secret place of His tent He will hide me; He will lift me up on a rock (Psalm 27:4-5).

Rabbit Pie

1 rabbit

water with 2 T. salt

Pie Shells

2 cups all-purpose flour, sifted
1 tsp. salt
4 T. butter

6 T. shortening (Crisco preferred)
6 T. milk

Filling

1 10.5-oz. can mushroom soup
8 oz. chicken broth (or water)
1 8-oz. pkg. frozen peas and carrots

2 cups potatoes, diced
salt to taste
pepper to taste

Cover the rabbit in saltwater and refrigerate overnight. Remove rabbit from saltwater and rinse well in clean water.

Place the rabbit in a Crock-Pot and cook until tender on medium heat. This can take 3 to 4 hours. Don't add salt until meat is cooked to keep it tender. Cook rabbit until the bones can be removed easily.

Take rabbit out of pot and remove the bones. (This is a good time to double-check to make sure all buckshot is removed). Break into bite-sized pieces, put into a pan, and set aside.

Pie Shells

Sift flour and salt together into a medium-sized bowl. Cut in shortening and butter with a pastry blender or large fork. Add milk. Gently stir with fork until well mixed. Add more flour if needed for desired consistency.

Divide dough in half and form two balls. Place dough balls on a floured surface and roll out each ball until dough is thin and big enough to fit the pie pan.

Place one pastry shell in bottom of pie pan, gently conforming to the pan's shape.

Filling

To the meat, add the mushroom soup and broth. Heat thoroughly.

Cook the peas, carrots, and potatoes until tender and drain. Combine the veggies with the meat mixture. Add salt and pepper to taste.

Place all the ingredients in the unbaked pie shell. Cover with the second pie shell and crimp pastry edges together. Brush top with butter.

Bake at 350° for 30 minutes.

There's More Than One Way to Bag a Rabbit

IT WAS DECEMBER, THE YEAR BEFORE I TURNED 15. My friend Kenny and I were rabbit hunting the brushy banks of a creek in West Virginia. We both had single-shot, 20-gauge shotguns and held them ready to pull up and fire at any cottontail we hoped would jump any moment.

After an hour of walking while kicking frost-covered clumps of heavy grass without success at stirring up rabbits, Kenny decided to try the other side of the creek. He found a narrow spot where he thought he could jump from one bank to the other. The bank he was jumping from was higher than the other bank by about five feet. The creek was six or seven feet wide, making it necessary for him to back up to get a running start. He broke his 20-gauge open, ejected and pocketed the shell for safety's sake, and proceeded to make the flying leap.

Being quite the athlete, Kenny had no trouble clearing the water. When he touched down on the other side, he landed on a sizable clump of grass. As his boots connected with the earth, I heard an unusual squeal. I thought he'd knocked the wind out of himself or maybe sprained an ankle. Then I heard him yell, "Did you hear that?"

"Yeah! You okay?" I asked.

Kenny laughed. "Yeah, I'm okay but this big rabbit ain't doin' so good!"

My friend had landed squarely on one of the biggest rabbits we'd ever seen. The impact killed it outright. Its hiding place in the heavy grass was an unfortunate choice. Kenny had done something that only one in a million—make that one in two million—could do. He'd killed a rabbit with his boots. He proved there's more than one way to bag a cottontail. As it turned out, it was the only catch of the day.

Baked Wabbit

submitted by Evelyn Bledsoe

2 T. solid shortening	2 cups water
1 or 2 large rabbits, cut into pieces	salt
½ cup all-purpose flour	pepper

Melt shortening in a large, iron skillet. Roll the rabbit pieces in flour and place in the skillet. Brown on both sides. Remove the rabbit pieces and place them in a single layer in a small roasting pan. Add salt and pepper to your taste.

Pour drippings from the skillet into the roasting pan. Add the water. Cover the pan with a tight-fitting lid or place foil securely on top of the pan.

Bake for 2 hours at 350°.

Tip: Serve the rabbit hot along with Poor Man's Gravy (page 241) made with the drippings.

Rabbit on the River

by Alice Click (Annie's sister)

DURING RABBIT SEASON IN THE 1960S, Dad would load us kids into his old, one-ton truck that could go just about anywhere. He'd take us to the part of our property he called "The Kanawha River Bottom Farm." He would get into the back of the truck and hold the shotgun on the cab roof. Mother would drive around in the field, and before too long we kids would see a rabbit—sometimes several—highlighted by the headlights of the truck. Dad would take aim the best he could. BANG went the shotgun. He would jump down from the truck bed, retrieve the rabbit, and place it in a coffee sack.

Mother would drive around the field a few more times. Usually Dad would have a bagged half-a-dozen rabbits before the evening was over. These rabbits were plump from feeding on Daddy's crops. Arriving home with a truckload of sleepy kids, they would put us to bed and then the real work began. Mom and Dad butchered the rabbits. It would be midnight before they finished the messy job and put the meat into the freezer.

Admittedly, we kids never considered the legality of Dad's rabbit hunting method, but we know his heart was in the right place. He was feeding his family and ridding his farm of crop moochers. All that concerned us kids was what would happen when Mom got hold of the soon-to-be-yummy bunnies.

When it was time to cook the rabbits, Mom would thaw the meat and make her famous "Rabbit and Gravy" meal.

The Williamson Family, circa 1962. Annie is "Miss Hollywood" in the sunglasses.

Mama's Rabbit and Gravy

1 rabbit
dash of salt
1½ cups flour

salt and pepper to taste
¼ cup cooking oil

Cut the rabbit into pieces by separating it at the joints. Soak the meat in cold water with a dash of salt. Let it soak for a couple of hours if possible.

Put the rabbit in a fresh pan of water and bring to a slow boil. Remove rabbit and drain, saving the "rabbit broth."

Roll the pieces of rabbit in ½ cup of flour and season with salt and pepper. Heat the oil in a cast-iron skillet and add rabbit. Fry until meat is tender and cooked all the way through. Remove the rabbit and set aside.

Add 1 cup of flour to the oil in the skillet and stir, making sure it doesn't burn. Pour the rabbit broth into the skillet. Turn down the temperature, cook, and stir until mixture reaches gravy consistency.

Pour gravy over rabbit and serve.

Tip: Serve with mashed potatoes and Sylvie Biscuits (page 222).

Roasted Rabbit

1 rabbit
2 T. lemon juice
1 tsp. onion powder

1 tsp. garlic powder
nonstick cooking oil
3 T. butter, melted

Rub the surface of the rabbit meat with lemon juice, onion powder, and garlic powder.

Place meat on a greased rack in a shallow pan. Brush meat generously with melted butter. Cover loosely with foil or, if you prefer, place the rabbit in a well-greased roaster pan with lid.

Roast at 325° for 2½ hours or until desired doneness.

Rabbit Normandy

2 eggs
½ cup milk
½ cup flour
½ cup cornmeal
2 rabbits, cut into pieces

salt and pepper to taste
¾ cup bacon grease (or vegetable oil)
1 shallot (or onion)
2 cups apple cider

Beat eggs and milk in a bowl, and then pour into a shallow dish.

Put flour in one pie tin, and put cornmeal in another pie tin. Dip sections of rabbit in egg mixture, then flour, then cornmeal, and place on a plate. Sprinkle meat with salt and pepper to taste. Let set for 10 to 15 minutes.

In a large skillet, melt bacon grease over low flame. Brown the shallot and then remove it (the onion flavor is now in the oil).

Sauté the rabbit in bacon grease until well done. Reduce flame and pour the apple cider over the rabbit. Cover the skillet and simmer very slowly until liquid has been absorbed or evaporated.

SOUL FOOD

Jesus said to them, "My food is to do the will of Him who sent Me and to accomplish His work" (John 4:34).

SMALL GAME

SOUL FOOD

*In the wilderness He fed you manna which your fathers did not know,
that He might humble you and that He might test you, to do good for you
in the end. Otherwise, you may say in your heart, "My power and the
strength of my hand made me this wealth"* (Deuteronomy 8:16-17).

Part 3
FOWL

TURKEY

Tips for Cooking Game Birds

The flavor and quality of the dining experience when it comes to wild game birds is largely determined by the care given by the hunter after bagging the bird. Here are some suggestions to be assured of the best taste when cooking.

- Wild turkey should be bled and cleaned immediately after shooting. Be sure to remove the oil sacs at the base of the back near the tail.

- Double check the meat for bullets, shot, or pellets. Use your fingertips to detect any shot that might have fragmented during the kill.

- Keep the meat cool until cooking. If desired, freeze the birds while they are fresh and in top condition using materials designed for keeping meat properly frozen. Remove as much air as possible from the bird meat package when sealing for the freezer. Keep meat at 0° or lower. Make sure you use meat within 6 months of freezing.

- Before cooking, trim off all fat.

- Dry cooking methods, such as frying, grilling, and broiling, are good for young birds.

- Moist cooking methods, such as stewing, baking, and braising, are best for older birds.

- To prevent skinned or older birds from drying out during baking, wrap each piece with a strip of bacon. The age of the wild turkey makes a difference in cooking preparations. The way to determine age is in the length of its spurs. Located on the inside of the legs about 3½ inches above the feet, young birds have short, dull spurs while older birds have long, sharp spurs. The older the bird, the tougher the meat. When cooking an older turkey, sprinkle commercial tenderizer in the body cavity and refrigerate for 12 to 24 hours.

FOWL

I Love the Wild Turkey!

I'**LL NEVER FORGET THE FIRST TIME** I stood at the microphone as a keynote speaker at a church-sponsored wild game dinner. I said, "I love wild turkey!" When I said it, I heard some gasps in the room. I wasn't sure why, and I paused for about two seconds to process the unexpected reaction. Then I suddenly realized there is a potent whiskey on the market called Wild Turkey. Convinced that there were those in the room who might be familiar with the "golden fire water," I immediately attempted to halt any fears and potential rumors.

"Let me rephrase my statement: I love *the* wild turkey—the bird!" I was relieved to hear laughter. And since it garnered such a response, I've been guilty of using that same line at events where hunters are present. I do it for the chuckle and to get a feel for my audience.

Seriously, I *really* enjoy chasing turkeys—big time! If you were to ask me which I like better: deer or turkey hunting, I would reply, "They're both on the same line." But in the category of which critter requires the least effort to get it home, the turkey wins wings down. And if you were to ask which is easier to process, then I'd guess you've never killed a deer and a turkey. It takes about ten minutes to properly remove the edible meat from a turkey compared to upwards of two hours to field dress a deer (at least the way I do it).

While the yield of venison is worth the work (in Tennessee the outcome is, on average, 35 to 55 pounds of meat), an average turkey in our area might yield 2 to 4 pounds of meat. Though much less in yield, turkey is just as exciting to cook and tasty to consume.

The following recipes are not only delicious, they also provide a way of honoring the legacy of wild turkey...the bird, that is.

"Gobble It Up" Wild Turkey

6 cups turkey breast, cooked
and diced
3 cups bread crumbs
¾ cup celery, chopped
1 onion, chopped
½ cup butter

½ tsp. poultry seasoning
1 egg, beaten
¾ cup milk
1 10.5-oz. can cream of
mushroom soup

Place turkey in a 9 x 13 rectangular baking pan.

In a skillet, sauté bread crumbs, celery, and onion in butter. Add poultry seasoning, egg, and milk. Spoon the mixture over the turkey. Pour and spread mushroom soup over the top.

Bake uncovered at 350° for 45 minutes.

SOUL FOOD

He has made My mouth like a sharp sword, in the shadow of
His hand He has concealed Me; and He has also made Me a select arrow,
He has hidden me in His quiver (Isaiah 49:2).

The Double Take

A JOYFUL HEART IS GOOD MEDICINE" (Proverbs 17:22). When I hunt with my friend Don Hicks, I usually leave him with my heart light and my soul nurtured. Why? Because we seem to do more laughing than hunting. And believe me, we do a lot of hunting at his place. While every visit is memorable, one of the best involves a spring gobbler hunt in a small pop-up blind best occupied by one person—but we were both crammed inside.

Sunrise came around six-thirty, and by eight we already experienced a morning of out-of-control laughter at everything from how pitiful our turkey-calling skills were to the silly twists we put on the old songs we were singing. Our sides were aching as we amused ourselves while trying hard to keep the hilarity down to a low roar.

Then Don took a look outside, and his eyes got bigger than fried turkey eggs. He pointed out the small window. "Steve, there's a huge gobbler right in front of us. Take it!"

We scrambled to put on ear protection. The unexpected, "out of nowhere" appearance of the big bird brought on some major preshot jitters for me. As if the sudden chaos inside the tiny tent was not enough to challenge my attempt to hold my shotgun steady, all of a sudden Don slipped off his little stool, dropped to his knees on the grass inside the blind, and curled up tightly in a strange position. I had no idea what he was doing, but it sure looked like he was praying. I knew if I laughed like I wanted to at the sight of this supposed intercessory moment on his part I'd never close the deal on the gobbler. So I focused on putting the bead on the bird. (I found out later Don wasn't interceding at all. He was trying to make room for me to maneuver my 12-gauge to the little window so I could take the shot.)

When I pulled the trigger, the concussion from the heavily loaded 3½-inch shell nearly threw the lightweight blind off of us. Before the report of the shot faded to silence, Don was up on his knees looking out the window to see if I'd connected. When he looked, his eyes widened again. He whispered excitedly, "There's another bird out there! Where's my gun?"

As he scrambled for his gun, I quickly peeked out the window. Sure enough, there was a second nervous gobbler going in circles around his friend who had, as far as he was concerned, suddenly exploded. I figured the second bird was saying, "Dude, if that's what springtime love does to a feller, you can count me out!"

Unfortunately for the lingering gobbler, while his attention was focused on his friend, he didn't notice the two of us shifting around inside the blind. Undoubtedly we looked look like Houdini trying to escape from a huge canvas sack. If the bird had, he could have made a lifesaving exit from the area. However, he stayed around long enough for Don to stick the barrel of his gun out the window and touch off a shot. And when Don pulled the trigger, I was on my knees inside the tent wadded up in the prayer position.

Within 20 seconds of the first shot fired, we had two birds outside the tent. With our kills separated by such a small number of seconds, we both agreed that this qualified as a "double kill." After a very, very short pause filled with us staring at each other in awe at what had just happened, we broke into full-volume frivolity and unrestrained congratulations.

What a huge relief to be able to open up with our laughter. We'd spent the morning trying so hard to suppress our noise that we were worried we'd be going into cardiac arrest. As we lifted the super-lightweight blind off us and cast it aside, we stood unhidden before our feathered targets. They were still doing the death dance that happens after birds are killed, which told us we needed to hurry over and pin them down. Without hesitation, we took off toward the birds.

Both gobblers were about the same size, and there wasn't a way to tell which of us shot which bird, but it didn't matter. We knew they were big enough specimens that when laid side-by-side, the double take would get a double take from all onlookers. We couldn't wait to get them home and sit down to a tasty reward for our morning's "work."

Doris Hicks, Don's sweet wife, knows how to turn a "double take" into a delicious dinner. You'll enjoy her recipe for turkey medallions!

Doris's Fried Turkey Medallions

1 wild turkey breast	salt and pepper to taste
½ cup flour	¼ cup cooking oil
½ tsp. cayenne pepper	honey mustard (or other dipping
Herbes de Provence mix*	sauce, see page 249)

Cut the turkey breast into 2-inch-wide sections. (The yield for each side of an average turkey breast will be approximately two 8-inch sections).

Roll the sections inside wax paper and freeze until almost solid to make for easy slicing. Cut the cooled sections of turkey into ½-inch slices (should yield 16 to 20 medallions).

Mix flour and cayenne pepper together.

Rub turkey with Herbes de Provence, roll meat in flour and cayenne mix, and then salt and pepper to taste.

Fry in cooking oil until lightly brown.

Serve hot with honey mustard for dipping.

* To make your own Herbes de Provence mix, combine these herbs:

3 T. marjoram, dried	1 tsp. basil, dried
3 T. thyme, dried	1 tsp. rosemary, dried
3 T. summer savory, dried	½ tsp. sage, dried
1 T. lavender, dried	½ tsp. fennel seeds

SOUL FOOD
*Bear one another's burdens, and thereby fulfill the
law of Christ (Galatians 6:2).*

Turkey Dressing Casserole

1 turkey breast
1 medium onion, chopped
2 stalks of celery, chopped
1 10.5-oz. can cream of
  mushroom soup

4 oz. milk
1 8-oz. container sour cream
nonstick cooking spray
1 12-oz. pkg. dry stuffing

In a large pot of water, cook the turkey breast, onion, and celery until tender.

Remove turkey from broth and cut into chunks. Strain the broth and set aside the onion and celery for the stuffing.

In a separate bowl, mix the soup, milk, and sour cream. Add the turkey and stir.

Pour the meat mixture into a greased casserole dish.

Prepare the stuffing according to package directions.

Add to the stuffing the onion and celery strained from the broth and spread over the turkey mixture.

Bake at 350° for 30 minutes or until the dish is bubbling and the stuffing is brown.

FOWL

Annie's Gold Nugget Wild Turkey

1 turkey breast
1 cup flour
1 tsp. salt
½ tsp. pepper

1 tsp. garlic powder
½ tsp. paprika
3 T. cooking oil (or butter)

Cut the turkey breast into 1-inch nuggets.

Combine flour, salt, pepper, garlic powder, and paprika. Dredge the turkey nuggets in the flour mixture.

Pour oil into a heavy skillet and heat to medium-hot. (If you use butter, which tastes yummy, make sure the temperature is not so hot that the butter burns.) Fry the nuggets until golden brown. Remove meat from skillet and place on a paper towel to drain excess oil.

Tip: Serve with Mom's Morels (page 213) and Homemade Dipping Sauce (page 249).

Wild Turkey Crock-Pot Supper

1 large turkey breast
3 cups chicken broth (or water)
1 15-oz. can cream of
   mushroom soup

1 15-oz. can cream of celery soup
salt and pepper to taste
Mrs. Dash's original seasoning

Place the turkey breast in a Crock-Pot. Add chicken broth and simmer for 2 hours.

Add mushroom and celery soups and continue to cook on low for 2 hours.

Add seasonings and, if needed, more water or broth to keep meat covered. Cook until tender.

SOUL FOOD

Let us draw near with confidence to the throne of grace, so that we
may receive mercy and find grace to help in time of need
(Hebrews 4:16).

Emmitt's First Turkey

WHEN EMMITT BEALL JOINED OUR FAMILY IN THE YEAR 2000 by marrying our daughter, Heidi, there were several things I immediately liked about the young man. Mostly, I liked that we had a lot in common. He's handsome, athletic, very intelligent, and a hard worker. (Okay, maybe we only have a few things in common...) People say girls grow up and marry men just like their daddies, which may be why mothers cry at weddings.

There was another thing I liked about Emmitt that I learned about later. Something Emmitt didn't even know when he got hitched to Heidi—but he certainly knows it now. He's a born hunter. And I'm happy to report that I helped him make the discovery! It happened one joyful spring when I suggested Emmitt join me for a gobbler hunt.

With his borrowed camo clothes, boots, and my old pump-action, 12-gauge Remington, Emmitt was ready to go. We arrived at the farm where we would hunt about 30 minutes before daylight. I set us up at the edge of a long field where I hoped turkeys would show up. Sure enough, about an hour after daylight we heard gobbling at the upper end of the field. A group of hens and bearded toms were coming our way. It wouldn't be too long before the boys in the flock would see my attractive hen decoy placed approximately 15 yards from us.

Believing the birds would appear over a little rise to our left, I instructed Emmitt to position his gun at a 90-degree angle from the decoy and put his finger lightly on the safety, ready to push it to the off position. But the birds fooled me.

Three gobblers decided to go around the little rise. That surprise put Emmitt in a predicament. To attempt a shot, he had to swing his gun to the right. I was sure a newbie hunter wouldn't be able to accomplish such a feat with three pairs of turkey eyes with their keen vision only 20 or so yards away. However, I noticed the birds were focused on the fake hen, so I quietly whispered to Emmitt, "If you think you can move as slow as a shadow on a sundial to get your gun around to one of those birds, go ahead and try it!"

What I saw next will always be one of the most amazing moments I've enjoyed while chasing turkeys. Emmitt began an incredibly slow and deliberate movement of his gun while releasing the safety. After at least a minute and a half of steady and sure maneuvering, he drew bead on one of the birds and pulled the trigger. The gobbler hit the ground. Emmitt jumped up and ran to his well-earned trophy.

I couldn't believe what I'd just seen. A first-timer had pulled off what many of us old-timers are still trying to do. How he managed to move so slowly with minimal noise, I'll never know. That day I knew my daughter had married a natural hunter.

Like I said, people say girls grow up and marry men just like their daddies...and that's why dads smile at weddings!

Emmitt, Heidi, and Steve ready to go hunting

Sweet and Sour Wild Turkey with Rice

1½ lbs. turkey breast
3 T. cooking oil
1½ cups water
1 20-oz. can chunk pineapple
   with juice
¼ cup brown sugar
2 T. cornstarch
¼ cup apple cider vinegar

2 T. soy sauce
½ tsp. kosher salt (kosher salt is
   purer, doesn't contain additives,
   and is milder than iodized table
   salt)
1 green pepper, cut into strips
1 onion, sliced thin
12 oz. rice

Cut the turkey into ½-inch cubes.

In a heavy skillet, heat the oil and then brown the turkey. (Do not drain the oil.) Add 1½ cups of water, cover, and simmer until the meat is tender, about 1 hour.

Drain the chunk pineapple, saving the juice for later.

Combine the brown sugar and cornstarch in a medium saucepan. Add the pineapple juice, apple cider vinegar, soy sauce, and salt. Cook until it starts to boil. Add the turkey meat. Cook until meat is done and sauce thickens, approximately 20 minutes. (If more liquid is needed, add a little bit of water.)

Add the pineapple, onion, and green pepper. Cook 3 to 5 more minutes until the vegetables are at desired tenderness.

Prepare rice according to package instructions.

Serve turkey over rice.

SOUL FOOD

[Jesus said,] "Do not fear; you are more valuable than many sparrows"
(Matthew 10:31).

FOWL

FOWL

Lessons from
the "Concession" Stand

SPRING TURKEY SEASON WAS IN FULL SWING IN TENNESSEE. Because I rarely pass up a chance to chase some birds, when my buddy Lindsey Williams called and asked if I wanted to join him the next morning for a hunt in his "Concession" stand (where we hide, eat, drink coffee, and wait for critters to show up), I answered yes before he could utter the last word of the invite. Before you start looking for a way to express your pity for my addiction to the chase, please understand that, for me, hunting is more than just providing meat for the table. There is an even more redeemable element to my obsession.

When I go hunting, it is also research. Each trip is an adventure into the fields of truth the Lord provides. Insights about relationships with Him and others, about His creation, and about myriad other things are highlights I enjoy discovering and including in my books. My hunt with Lindsey provides a good example of what can be discovered out there if a person is on the lookout.

About 30 minutes after daylight, Lindsey and I saw a hen wander into the huge meadow we were watching. She was about 200 yards from us. A minute or so later, we caught sight of two adult toms entering the field near the hen. Lindsey and I smiled as we silently encouraged the hen to move across the field toward us as she fed. However, it seemed she was about to lead the two gobblers away...but suddenly the two boys looked across the field in our direction and the game changed. What they saw was too much for their bird brains to resist.

Lindsey has a decoy called "B-Mobile." It's a life-sized strutting turkey that is painted in vivid detail. It sports a real turkey fan mounted in "full bloom." Next to B-Mobile, Lindsey had placed a hen decoy in a position that indicated being receptive to breeding. When the two amorous male birds caught sight of another male in full strut and about to close the deal with a hen, jealousy and desire took over.

The two mature gobblers did something that was actually out of character for birds their age. They turned their attention away from the hen in front of them and made their way across the field toward the two decoys.

The "real thing" they left alone seemed to look bewildered, offended, and miffed. Within a minute or so, the two lovesick and dangerously jealous gobblers closed in on B-Mobile. When they got closer, their emotions went completely out of control. Both of them gobbled simultaneously, loudly to say the least and forcefully enough that we nearly felt the wind from their angry rant. We're not sure what they said, but whatever it was, it would be their last words.

They proceeded to show fight as they neared and made several wide circles around B-Mobile. Just as they were about to attack their plastic counterpart, I heard Lindsey softly give the count-up. "One, two, three..." At three, the field rumbled with the report of two 12-gauge weapons of destruction. Instantly two toms paid a huge price for succumbing to jealous and covetous rage.

What was the takeaway from the field besides some really good eats? The obvious lesson gleaned from the two deceased birds is that a man should never ignore the deadly danger of yielding to jealousy. He should always heed the warning found in commandment number 10: "You shall not covet your neighbor's wife" (Deuteronomy 5:21). It's not a safe thing to do!

Blessings on your hunting and research. Each time you go, may you too find meat for your body and soul.

Lindsey's concession stand: Pass the cream, sugar, and shotgun, please!

Poached Turkey Breast

Poached turkey doesn't mean stealing one from your neighbor's land. Nope. We're talking a good way to prepare a turkey breast for eating or to use in other recipes.

1 skinless wild turkey breast, rinsed and patted dry	2 bay leaves
1 large onion, chopped	2 T. salt
3 carrots, chopped	1 tsp. whole black peppercorns
	6 T. distilled white vinegar

To determine ideal amount of liquid needed for poaching, put turkey breast in a deep pot and add enough cold water to cover by 1 inch. Now remove the turkey, leaving the water in the pot.

Put onion, carrots, bay leaves, salt, peppercorns, and vinegar in the pot. Bring to a boil.

Carefully put turkey breast into pot to avoid splashing. Reduce heat to a bare simmer.

Cook covered for 1¼ hours.

Remove from heat and let turkey cool in the liquid, uncovered, for 30 minutes. Drain and discard solids.

Serve cold or at room temperature.

FOWL

SOUL FOOD
The fruit of the righteous is a tree of life, and he who is wise wins souls
(Proverbs 11:30).

Lemon Marinated Wild Turkey Breast

1 poached wild turkey breast (see Poached Turkey Breast, page 159)

Lemon Marinade

1 lemon	1 tsp. salt
1/3 cup golden raisins	1/2 cup olive oil
3 T. lemon juice, fresh	2 T. capers drained
1½ tsp. balsamic vinegar	

Cooking Instructions

3 T. pine nuts	1 T. mint, fresh, chopped
1 T. parsley, fresh, chopped	

Marinating Instructions

Place poached turkey in a ziplock bag.

Carefully peel lemon, being careful to avoid the white part of the rind, which is extremely bitter. Cut peel into ½-inch strips and set aside.

Soak raisins in boiling water for 5 minutes. Drain and set aside.

In a small bowl, whisk lemon juice, balsamic vinegar, and salt together. Gradually pour olive oil into mixture, whisking to emulsify (thicken). Stir in lemon zest strips, raisins, and capers.

Pour liquid mixture into ziplock bag with turkey. Marinate chilled for 4 hours or overnight.

Cooking Instructions

Toast pine nuts by placing them in a dry skillet. Cook on medium heat until nuts are brown, stirring constantly. Set aside.

Remove turkey from marinade, setting the liquid aside. Cut turkey breast, on the diagonal, into ¼-inch strips.

Stir parsley and mint into marinade.

Place turkey on serving plate and spoon marinade dressing over meat. Sprinkle with toasted pine nuts. Serve cold or at room temperature.

SOUL FOOD

The word of God is living and active and sharper than any two-edged sword, and piercing as far as the division of soul and spirit, of both joints and marrow, and able to judge the thoughts and intentions of the heart (Hebrews 4:12).

QUAIL

Cooking Tips for Quail

- Serving size: Allow 1 to 2 quail per person

- Be careful to not overcook quail meat. It will become dry and tough. When is quail cooked properly? When the meat is slightly firm to the touch, similar to cooked chicken breast, and when the juices are clear.

- To determine whether a game bird is young and tender, the answer is as close as its bill. The stiffness of the bill is usually a good indicator. Lift the bird by its lower jaw. If nothing breaks, it's probably a mature bird. Because older birds tend to not be as tender as younger ones, you may need to adjust the recipe by marinating and cooking the meat a bit longer. Or you might choose a moist cooking method, such as stewing, baking, or braising.

Grilled Quail

4 quail
marinade (See "Gravies, Marinades, and Sauces," page 239, or try Newman's
   Own Marinade)
nonstick cooking spray

Place quail in a large ziplock bag. Add enough marinade to cover meat. Refrigerate for at least 8 hours, turning occasionally.

Coat the grill with nonstick cooking spray. Grill quail for 15 minutes per side, basting with the marinade.

Leavell Quail with Rice and Gravy

20 quail, ready to cook
½ cup Cavender's All-purpose Greek
  Seasoning
1 cup all-purpose flour
½ cup canola oil

⅛ cup water
1 cup milk
salt and pepper to taste
1 box instant brown rice

Season both sides of the quail liberally with Cavender's seasoning.

Dredge quail in ½ cup of flour and place in a large iron skillet with hot canola oil ⅛-inch deep. Cook until brown, 2 to 3 minutes. Turn over and brown other side. Do not drain skillet.

Turn heat to low. Add ⅛ cup of water, cover loosely, and simmer, steaming the meat until tender. Remove quail to a warming plate.

Loosen drippings from the bottom of the pan. Add oil if more liquid needed and heat until hot. Add ½ cup flour and stir, cooking until brown. Add milk, stirring constantly. When consistency is like gravy, remove from heat. Salt and pepper to taste.

Prepare rice according to package instructions.

Serve quail and gravy over the brown rice.

SOUL FOOD

*For you who fear My name, the sun of righteousness will
rise with healing in its wings* (Malachi 4:2).

Fried Quail

3 cups buttermilk	8 quail, whole
2 T. seasoning salt	2 cups all-purpose flour
2 T. hot sauce	peanut oil
1 T. garlic, minced	

In a large bowl, combine half the buttermilk with your favorite seasoning salt, hot sauce, and minced garlic. Mix thoroughly.

Add quail to buttermilk mixture and refrigerate for 4 to 24 hours.

Put flour in a ziplock bag. Dredge quail in the flour a few pieces at a time.

In a separate bowl, pour the remaining buttermilk. Dip the floured pieces of quail into the buttermilk. Once again, dredge the quail pieces in the flour. Place the coated pieces on a rack and allow to rest for 5 to 10 minutes.

In a large, heavy pot, heat peanut oil that is 4 inches deep to a temperature of 325°. Gently add quail (to avoid splatter). Fry until meat is golden brown and floats to the top of the oil. This should take 5 to 8 minutes.

Allow cooked quail to drain on paper towels before serving.

Tip: Serve with Three Corn Casserole (page 211).

FOWL

Quail with Chitterlings

2 quail (including intestines, liver, gizzard)	½ cup onion, chopped
salt	3 T. bacon drippings (or 3 T. cooking oil)
pepper	

Take the chitterlings (intestines) of two fat, full-grown quail and empty them of their contents under running water. Open them with a sharp knife and scrape off the inner coat. Wash them carefully.

Boil the chitterlings with the liver and gizzard. Add salt and pepper to taste. Add chopped onion. When meats are tender, set them aside to cool.

Put some bacon drippings into a skillet and fry the quail to a nice brown.

Tip: Serve with Poor Man's Gravy (page 241). This recipe also works with other types of fowl.

PHEASANT

A Pheasant Experience

WHEN THE PLANE LANDED IN DES MOINES, IOWA, my son, Nathan, and his friend Joey were giddy with anticipation for the hunt we were about to enjoy. I was just as excited. It was our first-ever pheasant hunt. And to top it off, we had a personal guide—a local farmer who owned a great bird dog. We were pumped!

By midafternoon our host was parking his truck along a paved country road near his farm and opening the doors for us and his fine pointer. We grabbed our trio of 12-gauge shotguns, loaded them, and were ready to head into the field with our new friend. But before we left the truck, we received some important instructions from our host.

"Guys, I can't tell you how glad I am that you're here. I've looked forward to showing you a good time. I know this is your first pheasant hunt, so I have to let you in on some rules of the game."

We didn't utter a sound as our tutor continued.

"There are just three things I want you to remember. First, don't take a shot unless you first quickly check to make sure humans are not standing beyond your barrel. I don't want to be interrupting our hunt with yanking buckshot out of somebody. Two, be mindful of where the dog is at all times—especially when you pull the trigger. A dead dog can end a lively hunt real quick. Third, if you hear me say "hen," don't you dare pull the trigger. We can't shoot hens here in Iowa, and if somebody happened to see us do it, I'd be in a heap of trouble."

He paused and looked at each one of us. "You boys got all that?"

Like good soldiers we barked a respectful, "Yes, sir!" And with that we were on our way into the field to hunt rooster pheasants.

The orange-and-white Brittany was totally engaged in the hunt and ran around like he was happy to be alive. Nathan, Joey, and I had our shotguns resting on our hips as we walked side-by-side about 25 yards apart, ready for the first pheasant to fly up. Suddenly, right between Nathan and Joey, a bird lifted off. The "whoofing" of the wings was a unique and rather loud announcement that a bird was ascending. Then we heard a yell from our host: "Hit it!"

With that command, Joey threw his gun up to his shoulder, pointed it in the direction of the flying feast, and pulled the trigger. Instantly the pheasant folded its wings and crashed to the earth about 30 yards from us. We three hunters were laughing and smiling, but our joy quickly turned to horror when we realized our host was marching toward us with a livid look on his face.

"Boys! We're right here by a road, and you killed a hen. I was sure I said you can't kill a hen! Didn't you hear me say 'hen'?"

The three of us looked at each other. Our expressions said what we were all thinking, but Joey vocalized our thoughts: "Sir, didn't you say 'Hit it'?"

That's exactly what I thought I'd heard, and I was sure Nathan heard that too. But boy were we wrong!

"No, son," the farmer said. "I said 'hen'!"

Joey then politely asked a question that didn't elicit a timid answer. "Is there any way you can say something else? Like "Don't shoot—it's a hen?"

Our host's response didn't get a challenge from us. "Boys, for more than 30 years I've been saying 'hen' when it's a hen, and I ain't changing things now. You're just gonna have to listen better."

I'm happy to report that not one more illegal bird fell to the ground on that trip. And we managed to take several legal birds. Even more important, each one of us took something home from Iowa that we still use to this day. The three of us are better listeners!

Nathan and Joey
Don't these guys look like a ton of fun to be with?

Slow-cooker Pheasant over Rice

Tip: Typically, one pheasant will feed three people.

2 T. olive oil	½ T. poultry seasoning
2 garlic cloves, minced	1 tsp. salt
¼ cup onion	1 tsp. pepper
1 pheasant, cut into small pieces	½ cup sour cream
(or 3 lbs. of small birds)	2 T. flour
1 cup chicken broth	1 cup milk
2 T. brown sugar	12 oz. rice

Put olive oil in a large skillet and heat. Sauté garlic and onion until they are transparent. Remove garlic and onion, leaving the oil.

Brown the meat pieces in the oil. Add the garlic and onion.

In a separate bowl, mix the chicken broth, brown sugar, and seasonings. Pour over the meat and heat thoroughly.

Pour skillet contents into a slow cooker. Cook on high until the bird is tender and falls off the bone, approximately 3½ hours.

Remove the bird, debone, and set meat aside.

Put the sour cream, flour, and milk into the liquid in the slow cooker and stir. Add the meat, and cook on low until broth is thick, approximately 1 hour.

Prepare rice according to package instructions.

Serve pheasant on a bed of rice.

SOUL FOOD

Blessed are those whose lawless deeds have been forgiven, and whose sins have been covered. Blessed is the man whose sin the Lord will not take into account (Romans 4:7-8).

FOWL

Crispy Pheasant

2 pheasants, butterfly cut	salt and pepper to taste
3 T. butter or margarine	¼ lb. bacon, cut in strips

Rub the pheasants with butter and then salt and pepper to taste.

Put the birds in a buttered casserole dish. Place the bacon on top of the birds.

Bake at 400° for 1 hour or until crispy and golden brown, basting with the buttery juices often.

SOUL FOOD

Having been justified by faith, we have peace with God through our Lord Jesus Christ (Romans 5:1).

DUCK

Duck Cooking Tips

- Ducks and geese should be plucked rather than skinned to retain flavor and moisture during cooking.

- Some people think waterfowl meat tastes best when it is aged. To age, hang the duck in a cool, dry area for 24 to 48 hours before cutting up. Try it and see how you like it. Check online for more ideas, suggestions, and instructions for aging meat.

- Older ducks and geese can be marinated in a solution of ½ teaspoon salt and 1 tablespoon vinegar per quart of cold water for 4 to 12 hours in the refrigerator. You may want to skin those birds that have had a diet of aquatic vegetation and animals.

- Fish-eating ducks (those with pointed or serrated bills) are best marinated before cooking. Use a marinade high in acid, such as lemon, lime juice, vinegar, wine, or buttermilk to remove any fishy or gamy taste.

- In the fall, ducks have a more desirable flavor than at other times of the year. If you are put off by the strong game flavor of some ducks, try soaking the meat in a bath of fairly strong salt water with a teaspoon of baking soda for a few days. Freezing a bird for a week or two will also help tenderize it.

Pan-fried Duck Breast Nuggets

4 duck breasts, cut into 1-inch strips
1½ cups water with 2 tsp. salt
½ cup canola cooking oil
2 T. butter
1 cup all-purpose flour

2 tsp. dry steak seasoning
salt
pepper
dipping sauces (see Gravies, Marinades, and Sauces, page 239)

Marinate the duck breast in saltwater for 36 to 48 hours. Remove from marinade and pat dry with paper towel.

Dredge duck in flour.

In a heavy skillet, combine the cooking oil and butter using medium heat. Fry the duck meat 3 to 5 minutes on each side, cooking to medium rare or desired doneness. (Do not overcook or meat will dry out.) Salt and pepper to taste and add steak seasoning.

Serve immediately with dipping sauce.

Grilled Duck Breast Salad

3 to 4 duck breasts

Marinade

¾ cup Italian salad dressing   ¼ cup Dale's Seasoning

Salad Ingredients

2 T. butter
1 cup pecans, chopped
1 head romaine lettuce, washed,
   broken into pieces

1 cup sweetened, dried cranberries
   or Craisins
1 cup Sweet and Sour Sauce
   (page 248)

Put the duck pieces in a large ziplock bag.

Mix together the Italian dressing and Dale's Seasoning. Pour into bag of duck breasts and marinate overnight in the refrigerator.

Remove duck breasts from marinade and grill over medium-hot fire, 4 minutes per side. (Do not overcook.) Meat should be a little pink in the center when done.

Chill the meat in the refrigerator until thoroughly cooled.

Thinly slice duck breast and set aside.

Melt butter in a skillet. Add pecans and cook until toasted, approximately 2½ minutes. Remove pecans from skillet and place on paper towels to drain and sit until cool to the touch.

In a large bowl, toss the lettuce, cranberries, and pecans.

Lay slices of grilled duck on top of the greens. Pour sweet-and-sour dressing over everything and serve.

SOUL FOOD

We preach Christ crucified, to Jews a stumbling block and to Gentiles foolishness, but to those who are the called, both Jews and Greeks, Christ the power of God and the wisdom of God. Because the foolishness of God is wiser than men, and the weakness of God is stronger than men
(1 Corinthians 1:23-25).

FOWL

Duck Gumbo

Our friend LaBreeska Hemphill provided this delicious recipe. When she sent this to us, she also included this note:

> I love to fish. I have a few big-finned trophies on the wall alongside my husband Joel's trophy catches. I've reeled in several large bass out of Lake Guerrero in Mexico. But being married to a hunter and living in Louisiana, I've learned to cook big and small game. Of all the meals I do with wild game, duck gumbo is my favorite. I've made it often when we've had gatherings at the house, and it hits the bull's-eye every time.

Making Duck Gumbo

3 ducks	½ tsp. salt
1 chicken breast	½ tsp. pepper
1 lb. smoked sausage, chopped	¼ tsp. cayenne pepper
2 bunches green onions, diced	1 T. Filé (powdered seasoning)
1 bell pepper, chopped	6 oz. okra, chopped
6 stalks celery, chopped	1 1.25-oz. pkg. Creole gumbo mix
½ cup flour	1 12-oz. pkg. of rice

In a very large pot or kettle, boil duck and chicken meat until done. Let cool and remove skin and bones. Put the meat back into the liquid (stock).

In an iron skillet, brown the sausage and drain. Add to stock.

Sauté onions, bell pepper, and celery in sausage drippings. Add to stock, keeping some of the oil in the skillet.

Add flour to the remaining sausage drippings in skillet and brown. Add to stock.

Add salt, pepper, and cayenne pepper to stock.

Add okra and bring to a boil.

Prepare rice according to package instructions.

Add Filé to the stock just before serving, stirring very little.

Serve the duck over the hot rice.

DOVE

Let Dove Season Begin!

FOR THE HUNTERS IN OUR STATE OF TENNESSEE, as well as many other states in our region of the country, September first is considered a red-letter day. Typically it's on or about that date when dove season starts. Why is this so special? Very simply, most of us have spent a long summer separated from the fair chase by the laws that govern our legal right to harvest game. Because turkey season ends in early May, by the time dove season arrives, we're clawing at the ground to get outdoors to hunt.

The evidence that we're stoked and ready to feed our hunger for the hunt can be seen and heard on farms that have fields where doves live, eat, and roost. Hunters by the thousands go to the fields early that first morning. Encompassing all ages, men and women take their seats on portable stools and lock and load their weapons.

I've been on my share of dove hunts, and usually the more popular hot spots are crowded with hunters. We sit within a few yards of each other and blast away at the speedy birds that seem to fly by as fast as a small Cessna. Because they are such tiny targets and hard to bring down, their quick flight down the field creates a sight and sound that is most unique. Like a human wave that a crowd makes in the stands of a football stadium, shooters raise their guns in succession to take their turns at the birds that jet by.

I'm amazed at how many birds get to the end of a field unharmed. Of course, there are a few hunters who are crack shots and bring a halt to the "wave" moving down the field. However, most of the hunters are like me. When it comes to dove hunting, I estimate we average about a dozen shells per bird.

When the doves aren't flying, most of us are digging into our camo coolers for soft drinks and ham sandwiches. More often than not, just about the time we take a bite of a tasty treat of salty ham on white bread lathered with mayo and graced with a juicy late-season tomato, someone yells, "Birds!" We toss down our food, grab our guns, and throw more buckshot. Once that section of the flock has made its way past us, we go back to shoving food into our mouths.

I might not have a lot of success at a dove field, but you can be sure that I have a silo full of fun. And the only thing better than a day of blasting at doves is eating them. Here are a couple of good recipes to help make the expense of all those shotgun shells worth the investment.

FOWL

Dove Casserole

6 doves	2 cups chicken broth
1 tsp. salt	¼ cup shortening (or vegetable oil)
½ tsp. pepper	1 T. self-rising flour
2 T. butter	8 oz. mushrooms, sliced and sautéed
1 small onion, sliced	2 T. ketchup
1 clove garlic, minced	2 T. sherry (optional)
1 bay leaf	12 oz. wild rice

Rub the doves with salt, pepper, and butter. Place in a casserole dish, along with the onion, garlic, bay leaf, and chicken broth.

Cover and bake at 350° until meat is tender, approximately 40 minutes. Remove birds from oven and casserole dish.

Melt fat in skillet on medium heat. Blend in flour. Slowly add liquid from casserole dish, stirring constantly. When liquid is thick, add mushrooms, ketchup, and sherry. Simmer a few minutes longer, allowing the flavors to mingle.

Prepare rice according to package instructions.

Serve doves over wild rice.

SOUL FOOD

[Jesus said,] "Whenever you fast, do not put on a gloomy face as the hypocrites do, for they neglect their appearance so that they will be noticed by men when they are fasting. Truly I say to you, they have their reward in full" (Matthew 6:16).

Dove Stroganoff

16 to 18 dove breasts, skin removed	½ cup white cooking wine or chicken broth
1 medium onion, chopped	¼ tsp. oregano
3 T. butter	¼ tsp. rosemary
1 10.5-oz. can cream of celery soup	1 cup sour cream
1 6-oz. can mushroom pieces	1 12-oz. pkg. noodles

Place dove breasts in a large baking dish.

Sauté onions in butter until translucent and put into a large mixing bowl. Add remaining ingredients, except sour cream, and mix thoroughly. Pour mixture over the doves.

Cover and bake at 350° for approximately 1 hour. Remove from oven, add sour cream, and stir. Return to oven and continue baking, uncovered, for 15 to 20 minutes.

Prepare noodles according to package instructions.

Serve dove mixture over noodles and enjoy!

SOUL FOOD

*O that I had wings like a dove! I would fly away
and be at rest* (Psalm 55:6).

FOWL

SOUL FOOD

Do not weary yourself to gain wealth, cease from your consideration of it.
When you set your eyes on it, it is gone. For wealth certainly makes itself
wings like an eagle that flies toward the heavens (Proverbs 23:4-5).

Part 4
FISH AND OTHER AQUATICS

FISH

Tips on Cooking Fish

- Fish with scales need to have the scales removed. "Scaling" is easier if vinegar is rubbed on the fish first.

- Rub oil on fish before grilling to keep the meat from becoming too dry.

FISH AND OTHER AQUATICS

Just Add Water

AS A DAD WHO IMMENSELY ENJOYS FISHING, when our children were very young I took them with me and learned an important lesson: If you want to be with your kids, take them fishing. *If you want to fish, don't take your kids.*

Trying to do serious fishing with kids around is almost impossible. Really, it's even downright dangerous. I struggled a bit with this reality, but thankfully I came to realize that having Heidi and Nathan with me was the point—not the fishing. For that reason, I didn't really mind that we'd get tangled up in the line or that I risked getting a hook embedded in my jaw or backside as a result of a cast gone astray.

Because I was determined to put our togetherness high on the list of importance than merely catching fish, I now have great memories to recall. And because I had ample opportunities to practice what I preach, I feel qualified to write this song lyric for dads who have young kids and an appreciation for angling. It's actually a recipe for some real fun!

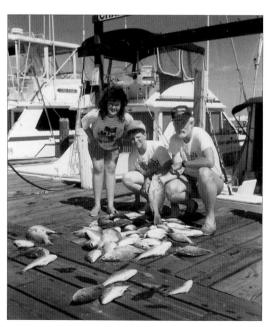

Heidi, Nathan, and Steve, Gulf of Mexico, 1988

JUST ADD WATER

If you want to make a sweet memory with your kids
here's the recipe
Peanut butter and a jar of jam
Loaf of bread and pop in a can
Bamboo poles and hooks on the line
Can of worms and some of your time
And don't forget that little round bobber
Then all you do is just add water

Just add water, don't have to be deep
Take 'em to the banks of a big lake or a little creek
Sweet memories with your sons and your daughters
That's what you'll get when you just add water

You can take your phone, but leave it off
Turn on your heart, and let it talk
'Cause words come easy when you're fishing
And when they talk, make sure you listen
If the weather turns hot and the fish go hide
Don't pack it up and run back inside
Just tell the kids, "Do like your father!"
Roll up your pants and just add water

Just add water, don't have to be deep
Take 'em to the banks of a big lake or a little creek
Sweet memories with your sons and your daughters
That's what you'll get when you just add water

RED SNAPPER

Red Snapper Jubilee

When our kids were younger, one of our choices for a fishing spot took us to a place where the water was much deeper than the creeks or lakes near our house. Heidi, Nathan, and I fished in the Gulf of Mexico out of Gulfport, MS. The red snapper were plentiful! After two days of arm-tiring tugging to bring in our catch, Annie used some great recipes to turn our hard work into a feast. This is one of her favorites.

2 red snapper fillets
butter-flavored cooking spray
4 T. butter
1 medium garlic clove, minced
3 to 4 drops Worcestershire sauce
½ tsp. Creole seasoning

$^1/_8$ tsp. ground black pepper
1 tsp. parsley, fresh, minced
1 tsp. chives, frozen or fresh
4 T. seasoned bread crumbs
2 T. Parmesan cheese, grated

Put red snapper fillets in a baking dish sprayed with butter-flavored cooking spray.

Melt butter in a cast-iron skillet. Add garlic, Worcestershire sauce, Creole seasoning, pepper, parsley, and chives. Cook at low heat for about 2 minutes.

Brush both sides of the fillets with the herb and butter combination. Sprinkle the fillets with the bread crumbs and Parmesan cheese.

Bake at 400° for 10 to 12 minutes (thickness of fillets determines baking time). When the fish flakes and is no longer translucent, it is done.

Tip: Serve with Chapman's Chin-lickin'-good Hush Puppies (page 223) and Coleslaw (page 208).

Perfect Pan-seared Red Snapper

2 fillets of red snapper (4 oz. each)	1 T. honey
1 T. olive oil	1 tsp. Dijon mustard
1 lemon, juiced	¼ cup green onions, chopped
2 T. rice wine vinegar	1 tsp. ginger, ground

Using cold water, rinse the snapper and pat dry with paper towels.

In a shallow bowl, mix the rest of the ingredients.

Heat a well-seasoned cast iron skillet on the stove using medium temperature. Dip snapper fillets in liquid mixture, coating both sides. Place in skillet and cook 2 to 3 minutes per side.

Pour remaining marinade into skillet. Lower heat and simmer for 2 to 3 minutes. When fish flakes easily with a fork, it is ready to serve.

SOUL FOOD

*If we have food and covering, with these we shall
be content* (1 Timothy 6:8).

FISH AND OTHER AQUATICS

COBIA

Heidi Holds the Record

WHEN NATHAN, HEIDI, AND I LEFT THE GULFPORT, MS, dock in the big charter boat, we didn't know the two-day excursion would end with the boys being totally out-fished by the only girl in the group. The cobia (Lemon fish) were running in the Gulf of Mexico, and we'd like to say "We wore 'em out," but the truth is they wore us out.

Nathan yanked for quite a while on a 42-pounder before landing it. I got into a nice 29-pound brute, fighting it for at least 20 minutes. We thought we were kings of the boat until Heidi hooked the big one. She sat strapped into a chair hanging on tight to what turned out to be a 54-pound cobia. She wrestled that monster for a good 40 minutes. I helped some, Nathan helped a little, but Heidi was the one who landed that whale of a fish. She deserves full credit! To this day she holds the record on the Chapman Family Wall of Fin Fame.

Heidi with cobia

Grilled Cobia with Lemon Pepper

1 cobia fillet, skinned	garlic powder
olive oil	fresh dill
lemon pepper	lemon juice

Lightly rub cobia fillet with olive oil. Sprinkle on lemon pepper and garlic powder to taste.

Start a charcoal grill, letting temperature rise very hot. Place fillet on grill, but not directly over the heat source. Cook for 6 to 7 minutes. Turn fillet and grill another 6 to 7 minutes, still over indirect heat.

Remove the cobia from the grill and allow it to rest, letting the juices settle. Sprinkle with fresh dill and lemon juice.

Tip: Serve with Homemade Tartar Sauce (page 250).

Nathan with fish

SALMON

Heidi's Wonderful Salmon

My all-time favorite fish to eat is salmon, and my favorite way to eat it is how my daughter, Heidi, makes it. There's something about the taste of wild salmon that tempts me to run everybody off so I can hoard all the fillets. Thankfully, Heidi usually makes more than enough to feed everyone—and often sends me home with leftovers!

INGREDIENTS

2 cloves of garlic, minced	1 tsp. ground black pepper
½ cup light olive oil	1 T. lemon juice, fresh or concentrate
1 tsp. dried basil	1 T. parsley, fresh, chopped
1 tsp. kosher salt	2 large salmon fillets

Preheat oven to 375°.

In a medium glass bowl, combine the garlic, olive oil, basil, salt, pepper, lemon juice, and parsley. Mix thoroughly.

Place salmon fillets in a separate glass bowl. Pour the liquid over the fillets, and marinate in the refrigerator for an hour, turning occasionally.

Remove salmon from marinade. Place the fillets in enough aluminum foil that the edges curl up to hold in liquid. Pour in all the marinade and crimp the edges of the foil to seal. Place the foil-covered salmon in a glass dish.

Bake at 375° for 35 to 45 minutes. You'll know the salmon is ready when the flesh easily flakes with a fork.

Tip: Serve with baked potato and Asparagus Tomato Supreme (page 207).

Salmon Cakes

1 14.7-oz. can pink salmon	½ cup milk
1 egg	1 cup flour
1 onion, finely chopped	¼ cup cooking oil

Optional
Homemade Tartar Sauce (page 250)
ketchup
Homemade Cocktail Sauce (page 249)

Empty the salmon into a small bowl. Add the egg, milk, and onion. Stir well.

Form into biscuit-sized cakes and roll in flour.

Fry in hot oil until golden brown.

Serve with tartar sauce, ketchup, or cocktail sauce.

SOUL FOOD

Oh give thanks to the LORD, for He is good, for His lovingkindness is everlasting. Let the redeemed of the LORD say so, whom He has redeemed from the hand of the adversary and gathered from the lands, from the east and from the west, from the north and from the south (Psalm 107:1-3).

TROUT

Lemony Trout Almondine

4 1bs. trout	2 T. butter
salt and pepper	¾ cup slivered almonds
¾ cup flour	1 T. lemon juice
2 T. olive oil	

Sprinkle trout with salt and pepper to taste. Dredge trout in flour.

In a skillet, heated to medium high, pour oil and 1 tablespoon of butter. Add fish and cook 3 to 4 minutes on each side until light brown.

Remove fish from the pan, cover, and keep warm.

Using the same pan, add 1 tablespoon of butter, heating to medium high. When the butter is melted, add the almonds and sauté. Add the lemon juice and heat through.

Place the trout on a serving plate. Spoon almond mixture over the fish and serve.

SOUL FOOD

I wait for the LORD, my soul does wait, and in His word do I hope.
My soul waits for the Lord more than the watchmen for the morning
(Psalm 130:5-6).

Easy Trout

2 trout fillets	1 tsp. salt
1 cup milk	½ tsp. pepper
¾ cup flour	1 stick butter

In a bowl, soak the trout fillets in milk for 5 minutes.

Combine flour, salt, and pepper.

Melt butter on medium heat. Fry trout until golden brown and the flesh of the fish flakes. Cook each side 3 to 4 minutes.

SOUL FOOD

God is our refuge and strength, a very present help in trouble. Therefore
we will not fear, though the earth should change and though the moun-
tains slip into the heart of the sea; though its waters roar and foam, though
the mountains quake at its swelling pride (Psalm 46:1-2).

CATFISH

Those Creepy Catfish...Mmmm!

by Annie Chapman

OF ALL THE FISH MY DAD BROUGHT HOME, my least favorite to see were the buckets of live, just-caught catfish. I guess it was the whiskers and the mean glint in their eyes that gave me pause. I gladly stood aside to let my brothers kill and clean the slimy things.

But when the cleaning work ended and the cooking started, my opinion of the creepy fish changed dramatically. Here are the recipes our family so enjoyed. They helped me get past the disconcerting expressions of the beady-eyed swimmers. I hope you enjoy them too!

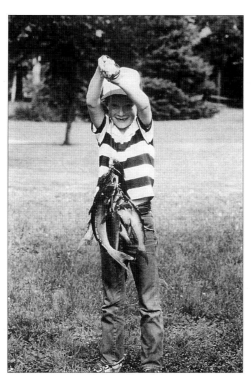

Nathan with catfish

Catfish Stew

2 10-oz. cans tomato soup
2 10-oz. cans water
1 16-oz. bottle ketchup
4 T. Worcestershire sauce
2 tsp. salt
1 T. black pepper

1 T. hot sauce
½ lb. bacon or salt pork
3 large onions, chopped
4 or 5 lbs. catfish (chunked or
    filleted)

Place the first 7 ingredients in a large pot and cook over low heat.

Dice the bacon and fry over medium heat. Remove bacon and sauté onions in the bacon grease until tender. Add to soup mixture.

Simmer for 30 minutes.

If desired, lightly salt the catfish. Add to soup mixture.

Simmer 12 to 15 minutes. When done, the fish should flake when tested with a fork.

Tip: Serve over steamed rice.

FISH AND
OTHER
AQUATICS

Fried Catfish

1½ T. salt
1½ T. celery salt
2 tsp. cayenne pepper
½ T. dry mustard
½ T. thyme
1½ T. paprika
1 tsp. black pepper
½ tsp. ginger, dry

2 bay leaves
½ cup flour
1½ cups cornmeal
catfish fillets, boned
1 cup milk
peanut oil (enough to be ½-inch
    deep in skillet)

Mix spices (first 9 ingredients) well and put in a large mixing bowl. Add flour and cornmeal and stir.

Pour milk into a shallow bowl.

Dip catfish in milk and then in the dry ingredients mixture.

In a deep skillet, heat peanut oil to 375°. Add fish and deep fry until golden brown.

Tip: Serve with Chapman's Chin-lickin'-good Hush Puppies (page 223) and Coleslaw (page 208).

Grilled Catfish

2 pounds catfish

Basting Sauce

1 stick butter, melted	2 T. Worcestershire sauce
$^2/_3$ cup lemon juice	1 tsp. salt
dash of hot sauce	1 tsp. ground pepper
1 tsp. mustard	1 tsp. chili powder

Wash the catfish meat in cold water and pat dry.

Whisk together basting sauce ingredients.

Place catfish on a well-oiled grill or grilling basket over medium heat or coals for approximately 20 minutes. While grilling, baste the catfish frequently with the sauce. Turn fish over and grill for another 15 minutes, continuing to baste often. When fish flakes easily with a fork it's ready.

Pecan-coated Fried Catfish

1 cup pecan pieces	1 cup cornmeal
1 cup buttermilk	1 tsp. salt
2 eggs	1 tsp. pepper
1 tsp. hot sauce	2 to 2½ lbs. catfish
½ cup flour	nonstick cooking oil

Toast the pecans by placing them in a dry skillet over medium heat. Stir constantly until pecans are golden brown. (Be careful because they burn easily and quickly.) Place the toasted nuts in a food processor and grind until the consistency of meal. Set aside.

In a shallow bowl, stir together buttermilk, eggs, and hot sauce.

In a separate dish, stir together flour, cornmeal, pecans, salt, and pepper.

Wash the catfish in cold water and pat dry. Dip the fillets into the buttermilk mixture and then into the cornmeal mixture. After coating each fillet well, set it aside on a piece of waxed paper until ready to cook.

Place fillets on a greased pan.

Bake at 350°degrees for 20 minutes or until meat is brown and flakes easily with a fork.

Tip: Serve with Chapman's Chin-lickin'-good Hush Puppies (page 223) and Coleslaw (page 208).

WALLEYE

Deep-fried Walleye

8 oz. (2 sleeves) saltine crackers
1 tsp. garlic powder
1 tsp. pepper
2 to 3 lbs. fresh walleye fillets,
    skinned (or yellow perch)

2 eggs
1 cup milk
corn or canola oil, 1-inch deep
    in skillet

Using a blender, grind the saltine crackers to almost flour consistency. Add garlic powder and pepper and mix well. Put in a shallow bowl or plate.

Cut fish into pieces and set aside.

In a large bowl, whip eggs with milk.

Dip pieces of fish in milk mixture, and then dredge in cracker flour, coating the fish well. Place fish on a paper towel-covered plate.

In a deep skillet, heat cooking oil to 400°. Carefully drop fish pieces into the hot oil.

Deep-fry fish 3 minutes per side (pieces will float when done). Remove fish from oil and place on several layers of paper towels to drain. Pat dry and serve.

SOUL FOOD

*"The bread of God is that which comes down out of heaven, and gives
life to the world"...Jesus said to them, "I am the bread of life;
he who comes to Me will not hunger, and he who believes in Me
will never thirst"* (John 6:33,35).

BASS

Battered Bass

2 cups flour	6 to 8 bass fillets, boned
1 cup cornmeal	1 cup milk
1 tsp. salt	½ cup vegetable oil
1 tsp. pepper	

Combine all dry ingredients in a large ziplock bag.

Pour the milk into a shallow bowl. Soak the fillets in milk for 1 to 2 minutes.

Removing one fillet at a time, place it in the plastic bag and shake, coating thoroughly.

Pour the vegetable oil into a heavy skillet and heat on medium-high. Put fillets in skillet, being careful not to crowd them. Fry until golden brown, approximately 4 minutes on each side. Remove from skillet and drain on paper towels.

Broiled Fish Parmesan

¼ cup milk (or buttermilk)	1 tsp. salt
1 lb. fish	½ tsp. pepper
2 T. Parmesan cheese	1 tsp. garlic salt
½ cup bread crumbs, dried	nonstick cooking spray
½ tsp. paprika	1 T. butter, melted

Pour milk into a medium-sized mixing bowl. Place the fillets in the bowl, coating each piece.

In a separate bowl, combine dry ingredients.

Dredge the milk-covered fillets in the dry mixture, coating each piece well.

Place the fillets on a baking dish sprayed with oil. Dribble melted butter on each piece of fish.

Broil at 425° for 15 minutes or until golden brown.

BLUEGILL

Lily's First Fish

ON A LATE AFTERNOON, OUR DAUGHTER, HEIDI, and her husband, Emmitt, along with their two daughters, were visiting our home. Evening dinner was three or four hours away, so I suggested we use the time to head out to the big lake at Coldstream Christian Camp near Adams, TN, for a quick wetting of fishing line. Our oldest granddaughter, Lily, jumped on the idea like it was a trampoline. (I'd bought three tubs of night crawlers at a local convenience store, fully expecting her thrilled reaction to the idea of going fishing.)

Within 45 minutes, Lily, Emmitt, and I were pushing off into the calm lake in one canoe, while Heidi was pushing off in another. Five minutes later we were fishing. I did the paddling and positioning near the known "hot spots," while Emmitt took care of the dangerous job of baiting Lily's hook as she held the rod and reel. He knew that one mischievous jerk of the pole by his loving daughter and he might be digging a barbed hook out of his hand. Fortunately for him, Lily was compliant with the policy of not moving when her daddy was pinching a hook between his fingers.

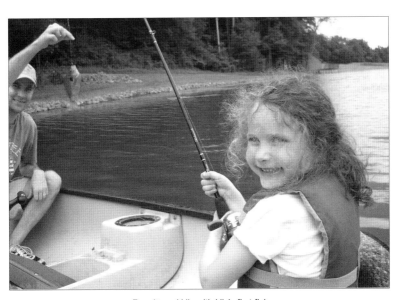

Emmitt and Lily with Lily's first fish.

I was thrilled to be within two feet of my precious grandgirl when the bobber on her line disappeared and she felt the tug through the pole for the very first time. Days just don't get any better than that!

Emmitt quickly encouraged, "Set the hook, Lily!" He'd schooled her on how to do it, and she was a quick study. Without hesitating, she sharply lifted the tip of her rod into the air. Suddenly the tip of the pole was dancing. Her eyes widened as she squealed with excitement. She cranked the reel handle, and within a few seconds she hoisted a bluegill out of the water. Her prize was a little bigger than her hand—a perfect first catch.

Emmitt reached for the line to steady his daughter's finned trophy, and that's when Lily turned to make sure her Papa—me!—was watching. I was indeed—through a camera lens. The following recipe is a tasty way to honor any kid's first catch. (Bear in mind that it takes several bluegill to make enough for a meal. But, hey, catching them is half the fun! The other half of the fun is eating them.)

Batter-fried Bluegill

ice-cold water
2 cups fry coating mix
3 cups peanut oil

1 lb. bluegill, filleted and boned
salt

Prepare the batter by mixing ice-cold water with the fry mix. (Ice-cold water helps the batter stick to the fillets.)

Pour peanut oil into a skillet and heat to 350° on medium-high.

Coat the fish with the batter evenly. (There will be some dripping.)

Place coated fish in the skillet and cook until golden brown, 2 to 3 minutes per each side.

Remove fish from oil and drain on paper towels. Season with salt and serve.

FROG LEGS

Jumpin' Frog Legs

3 T. cooking oil
6 to 8 frog legs

½ cup all-purpose flour
salt and pepper to taste

In a large iron skillet, heat oil to medium hot.

Coat the frog legs with flour.

Heat the oil in a large skillet. Put the frog legs in a single layer in the skillet. Fry slowly, turning once. (If needed, add a little more oil.) Sprinkle with salt and pepper after turning.

Cook for 15 minutes or until golden brown. (Do not overcook. You don't want the meat to fall off the bones.) Serve hot.

Tip: Keep the skillet lid handy. Sometimes as the legs heat, they jump as if trying to get out of the skillet!

Fried Frog Legs

2 eggs, beaten
2 T. mayonnaise
1 T. cornstarch
1 T. lemon juice
½ tsp. baking soda
1 tsp. salt

½ tsp. pepper
2 pounds of frog legs
2 cups canola oil
$2/3$ cup all-purpose flour
$1/3$ cup Italian bread crumbs

Combine the eggs, mayo, cornstarch, lemon juice, baking soda, salt, and pepper to use as a marinade. Pour into a large plastic ziplock bag.

Place frog legs in the marinade and seal. Refrigerate for 24 hours, turning the bag a couple of times to fully marinate the meat.

In a heavy skillet, pour in canola oil to 1-inch depth and heat to 350°.

Mix the flour and bread crumbs in a ziplock bag.

Remove the frog legs from the marinade, allowing the liquid to drain off. Dredge the legs in the flour/bread crumb mixture.

Fry the legs in the hot oil until golden brown, approximately 5 minutes per side, turning only once.

Tip: Serve with Becky's Potato Soup (page 217).

TURTLE

Wrestling River Farm Turtles

by Annie Chapman

IN MY OPINION, turtle falls into the category of foods that I call "Who in the world looked at that and said, 'I'm gonna kill that thing and eat it!'" I suppose the answer to that categorical question would be "Somebody who was really hungry." Obviously, turtle is not a first-choice dish for me. Still, there are many who don't require being near starvation to enjoy a serving of it. My dad was among those brave eaters. He not only loved to consume turtle, he liked finding them and bringing them home. My sister, Alice, six years my senior, shared with me some tense-filled memories of turtle hunting with Dad:

> As a 12-year-old girl, I recall going with my father to the back waters of the Kanawha River to capture a turtle so Mother could make one of Dad's favorite meals—turtle soup.
>
> It was along the tree-lined banks that the turtles preferred to hide. What a thrill to see a head bob up from time to time. Dad had figured out that he could tell the direction they were perched on the tree roots that were submerged under the murky waters by the way their heads rose above the surface.
>
> On this particular trip, after spotting a turtle about the size of the average automobile hubcap, my dad was about to take off his shoes and go into the creek. I, never fearing much of anything (including the snakes that called the creek home), announced I wanted to capture the shelled beast. Not hesitating, I proceeded to wade over to the turtle. As I pressed through the muddy bed of the creek in waist-high water, Dad cautioned that when I grabbed the turtle I should place my hands right on it, one on each side of the shell at its midsection.
>
> Once I reached the turtle I knew there was no turning back. When I grabbed the thing by the shell, the hind legs

violently thrashed. Being up close and personal to the sight of its sharp toenails, no one had to tell me that it was going to hurt really badly if they connected with my skin. I thought for a brief moment about tossing the heavy turtle out into the creek, but when I got a glimpse of the proud look on Dad's face, I was determined to hold on.

With the turtle's legs still swinging wildly, I wheeled around in the mud that sucked at my feet. I headed as fast as I could toward the bank. It felt like I was running through cold molasses. And holding the unhappy turtle at shoulder level was not easy either. After what seemed a full minute to make the short run to solid ground, I'll never forget the feeling of satisfaction when Dad smiled at my brave accomplishment. His joy was even greater when Mother transformed the ugly water crawler into one of Dad's favorite dishes that evening. We still refer to it as "N.R.'s River Farm Turtle Stew."

N.R.'s River Farm Turtle Stew

3 lbs. turtle meat
3 T. butter
3 T. flour
1 lb. onions, chopped
2 cloves garlic, chopped
1 4-oz. can tomato paste
3 T. canola oil
2 15-oz. cans tomatoes
¼ cup celery, chopped

1 cup green onion, chopped
1 cup bell pepper, chopped
⅛ tsp. cayenne pepper
4 bay leaves
8 cloves, whole
½ tsp. allspice
1 T. sugar
3 T. cider vinegar

Parboil turtle meat (put meat in a pot, add water to completely cover it, and boil for 10 minutes). Drain off water and let cool. Cut into pieces and set aside.

Make a roux: Combine butter and flour. Add onions, garlic, and tomato paste. Cook on low heat for 20 minutes.

Add the turtle meat to the roux, along with enough water to cover the meat. Cook until the liquid is reduced by half.

Add the remaining ingredients, stir, and cook for 30 minutes. Check to see if it needs more water to keep meat covered. Simmer for 3 hours.

Tip: Serve with Sylvie Biscuits (page 222).

FISH AND
OTHER
AQUATICS

ALLIGATOR

Alligator Alley

by Joel Hemphill

AS A NATIVE OF THE SOUTHERN AREA OF LOUISIANA where alligator is considered as edible as chicken, I always get a chuckle out of those who cringe at the thought of eating such a beast. But that's okay—it just leaves more for us Louisianans to enjoy. And if you're a gator eater, thankfully there are plenty to share.

Twenty-five years ago alligators were on the endangered list, but they've made a big comeback largely through the efforts of the Rockefeller Foundation. There's a huge wildlife and game refuge in South Louisiana that started allowing individuals to raise gators and harvest them, with the requirement that they release a certain amount into the wild. One 11-foot gator I bagged was estimated to be 75 years old. That long lifespan is rivaled only by some of Louisiana's large snapping turtles, which are known to live well over 100 years.

The annual gator season opens on the first day of September, and every year I look forward to hunting with my friends. The gator is still federally protected so hunting them requires a federal permit. Like other animals that are large, strong, and have a keen sense of self-defense, hunting alligators can be dangerous. But when hunted carefully and sensibly, it can be done without mishaps. Gator hunting is one of my favorite pursuits, not only for the challenge but also for the yield of fine meat to fill the freezer.

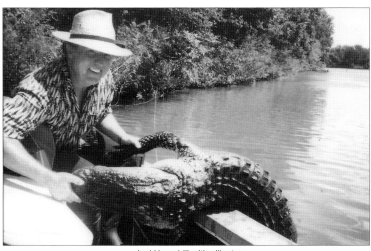

Joel Hemphill with alligator

FISH AND OTHER AQUATICS

203

Alligator Etouffee

submitted by LaBreeska Hemphill

1½ sticks butter	1 10.5-oz. can cream of
2 lbs. alligator, fat removed, cut into	mushroom soup
small pieces	1 10.5-oz. can cream of shrimp soup
1 bunch green onions	1 10-oz. can Rotel tomatoes
3 to 4 celery ribs, chopped	(with chilies)
2 onions, chopped	1 tsp. salt
2 bell peppers, chopped	½ tsp. black pepper
1 tsp. garlic, minced	½ tsp. red pepper
2 10.5-oz. cans cream of celery soup	Tony's Creole seasoning to taste

Melt 1 stick of butter in an iron pot. Add alligator meat, and sear until partially brown. Set aside.

Add in rest of butter and sauté chopped vegetables until wilted well. Mix the vegetables in with meat. Add the soups, Rotel tomatoes, and seasonings.

Simmer on low for 45 minutes or until meat is tender.

Tip: Serve over white rice and garnish with green onion tops.

FISH AND
OTHER
AQUATICS

Fried Alligator Tail

submitted by LaBreeska Hemphill

2 lbs. alligator tail	1 cup buttermilk
1 tsp. salt	½ cup flour
½ tsp. pepper	2 cups peanut oil

Cut alligator tail in small strips, and salt and pepper to taste. Dip in buttermilk and then roll in flour.

Heat peanut oil in a large skillet to 400°. Gently drop in meat. Cook for 3 to 5 minutes on each side or until meat is brown.

SOUL FOOD

*Many, O Lord my God, are the wonders which You have done,
and Your thoughts toward us; there is none to compare with You.
If I would declare and speak of them, they would be too
numerous to count (Psalm 40:5).*

Part 5
"SERVE WITH" SUGGESTIONS

VEGETABLES AND SALADS

Half Runner Green Beans

3 lbs. half runner green beans, fresh
3 beef bouillon cubes

2 T. bacon drippings (or vegetable oil)
¾ cup water

String and wash beans. Put green beans in a 6-quart pressure cooker. Add the beef cubes, bacon drippings, and water.

Put the lid on the pressure cooker and set for 15 pounds pressure. When the pressure gauge starts making noise, reduce heat and cook for 15 minutes.

Reduce the pressure in the pan by running cold water over the cooker in the sink to speed up cooling down process.

Asparagus Tomato Supreme

asparagus
cherry tomatoes
olive oil

salt
pepper

Trim off the woody stems of the asparagus and wash. Place on a large cookie sheet.

Place cherry tomatoes among the asparagus. Drizzle with olive oil, and salt and pepper to taste.

Bake at 350° until the asparagus is limp and the tomatoes are plumped up, approximately 20 minutes.

SOUL FOOD

Then God said, "Behold I have given you every plant yielding seed that is on the surface of all the earth, and every tree which has fruit yielding seed; it shall be food for you...I have given every green plant for food"
(Genesis 1:29-30).

Quick and Easy Salsa

1 28-oz. can diced tomatoes
1 10-oz. can Rotel tomatoes
1 onion, diced

1 bunch of cilantro, chopped
1 green pepper

In a food processor add all the ingredients and mix. Refrigerate and serve.

Coleslaw

1 head of cabbage
1 carrot
1 green pepper

salt and pepper to taste
Marzetti's Cole Slaw Dressing*

Shred or grate a head of cabbage into a bowl. Grate the carrot and green pepper into the bowl. Add salt and pepper to taste.

Add dressing until you get the consistency and taste you desire.

* You can also make your own dressing: 1 cup mayonnaise, 2 T. sugar, and 2 T. apple cider vinegar.

Broccoli and Cauliflower Coleslaw

"SERVE WITH" SUGGESTIONS

1 8 oz. pkg. shredded broccoli
    and cauliflower
½ cup cranberries
⅛ cup sunflower or pumpkin seeds

½ cup golden raisins
1 small red delicious apple,
    chopped
½ cup coleslaw dressing

Mix all ingredients and chill.

Tip: This is a nice variation on traditional coleslaw. Even though my family loves the simple shredded cabbage and mayonnaise coleslaw, they have come to appreciate the mixture of flavors in this twist on coleslaw. The green of the broccoli and the texture of the cauliflower adds visual and taste appeal.

Coleslaw Salad

1 8-oz. pkg. shredded cabbage
1 carrot, shredded
¼ cup cranberries
¼ cup sunflower or pumpkin seeds

¼ cup golden raisins
1 small red delicious apple, chopped
coleslaw dressing to taste

Mix all ingredients and chill before serving.

Green and White Salad

1 head cauliflower, broken into
  small pieces
1 head broccoli, chopped fine
16-oz. pkg. peas, frozen
8 slices bacon, fried and chopped
  into small pieces

¾ cup Miracle Whip or mayonnaise
1 cup sour cream
1 tsp. salt
1 tsp. sugar
4 to 6 green onions, cut fine
dash of garlic powder

Mix all ingredients together the day prior to serving. This salad keeps well in the refrigerator.

SOUL FOOD

[Jesus said,] "You are the salt of the earth; but if the salt has become tasteless, how can it be made salty again? It is no longer good for anything, except to be thrown out and trampled under foot by men"
(Matthew 5:13).

"SERVE WITH" SUGGESTIONS

Broccoli Cauliflower Salad

Dressing

½ cup light mayonnaise   1 T. vinegar
¼ cup sugar   1 T. garlic, minced

Salad

1 large head broccoli, chopped   8 slices bacon, fried crispy
1 small head cauliflower, chopped   4 oz. shredded Swiss cheese

Mix the first four ingredients to make the dressing.

In a separate bowl, combine the broccoli flowerets, cauliflower, bacon, and cheese.

Add dressing, toss, and chill before serving.

This salad can be made the night before so all the flavors have time to mingle.

You can also adjust how much dressing you use so you get the flavor without drowning the broccoli and cauliflower. This will save a few calories so you can have dessert!

SOUL FOOD

*There is an appointed time for everything. And there is
a time for every event under heaven...
a time to plant and a time to uproot what is planted*
(Ecclesiastes 3:1-2).

"SERVE WITH" SUGGESTIONS

Corn Casserole

This is a family favorite that seems to show up and show off nearly every time we get together.

4 large eggs	2 cans cream-style corn
2/3 cup safflower oil	nonstick cooking spray
1 tsp. garlic salt	½ cup cheddar cheese, grated
1 8.5-oz. box corn muffin mix	

Preheat oven to 375°.

Crack eggs into a large bowl and beat well. Add oil and garlic salt, mixing well. Stir in the dry muffin mix and cream corn until well blended.

Pour into greased baking pan, and sprinkle grated cheese on top.

Bake at 375° for 50 to 60 minutes or until brown, puffed on top, and the sides are slightly pulled away from the pan.

Remove from oven and let set 5 to 10 minutes.

Tip: Great served hot or at room temperature.

Three Corn Casserole

1 can whole-kernel corn, drained	1 stick of butter
1 can cream-style corn	1 8-oz. container sour cream
1 8.5-oz. box cornbread mix	nonstick cooking spray

Mix all ingredients and place in casserole dish sprayed with nonstick cooking spray.

Bake at 350° for 1 hour.

SOUL FOOD

Two things I asked of You, do not refuse me before I die: Keep deception and lies far from me, give me neither poverty nor riches; feed me with the food that is my portion, that I not be full and deny You and say, "Who is the LORD?" Or that I not be in want and steal, and profane the name of my God (Proverbs 30:7-9).

Great and Easy Baked Beans

2 lbs. White Great Northern
  beans, dry
1 40-oz. bottle ketchup
1 cup brown sugar
2 tsp. yellow mustard

1 small onion, chopped
10 slices bacon, fried and crumbled
2 T. bacon grease
red pepper flakes, dry

Wash the beans and remove any rocks and grit. Put them in a large kettle and cover with water. Bring to boil for 5 minutes. Pour off water, and refill with clean water. Bring to boil again.

Lower the heat and cook slowly until beans are almost done, but not soft. If needed, add additional water to cover the beans.

Put in most of the ketchup and brown sugar, all of the mustard, onion, bacon, bacon grease, and red pepper flakes.

Stir well and taste. If desired, add more ketchup and brown sugar. Add water if mixture is too dry to pour.

Pour the bean mixture into a 9 x 12 x 2 roaster or baking dish. Cover tightly with foil.

Bake at 350° for 1 hour. Remove the foil and bake for another 40 minutes or until beans are tender.

Tip: These baked beans are good served hot or cold.

"SERVE WITH" SUGGESTIONS

Morel Mushrooms

MY MOM AND BROTHER, NEY JR., loved to hunt morel mushrooms each spring. They seemed to have an internal sonar system that led them to the edible fungi. I accompanied the two of them on many occasions, trying my best to find the hidden delicacies, but I usually came home with an empty sack. While the umbrella-shaped mushrooms are a gastronomical treat, unless you're an expert at identifying mushrooms, don't pick them yourself. Some mushrooms that closely resemble morels are poisonous.

Mom's Morels

1 lb. morel mushrooms	1 tsp. salt
¼ cup cooking oil	½ tsp. pepper
½ cup flour	

Slice open each mushroom lengthwise and rinse well. Cut away the woody stub at the bottom of the stem. Be careful to handle the mushrooms as little as possible because they are quite delicate.

Add enough oil to a skillet to cover the bottom. Heat to hot, but not burning.

Turn each mushroom in a mixture of flour, salt, and pepper. Shake off the excess and gently place in skillet. Cook mushrooms until golden brown, turning once.

Remove from skillet and place on paper towels to drain. Serve hot, if possible.

Fireplace Baked Potatoes

baking potatoes
salt
butter

Use as many potatoes as you want,
and you don't need to wash them.
Bury the potatoes in the coals and let
them cook for 15 to 20 minutes. If desired, you can wrap them in foil.

Pull them out of the coals and poke with a fork to see if they're done (fork
should enter potatoes easily). If done, carefully wipe the skins clean.

Cut potatoes in half, add salt and butter, and serve hot.

SOUL FOOD
This is the day which the LORD has made; let us rejoice and be glad in it
(Psalm 118:24).

Mashed Potatoes

8 medium potatoes, washed and peeled	4 T. butter
½ tsp. salt	¼ cup milk
	½ cup sour cream

Cut potatoes into small chunks. Put into a 2-quart pan, add salt, and bring to boil. Cover and cook slowly until potatoes are tender, 15 to 20 minutes.

Strain out the water, add the butter, and cover until butter melts.

Use a hand mixer to mash the potatoes in the pan they were cooked in. Add milk and sour cream, and beat until creamy. Add more milk and butter until you get the texture you desire. Serve hot.

SOUL FOOD

[Jesus said,] "Come to Me, all who are weary and heavy-laden, and I will give you rest. Take My yoke upon you and learn from Me, for I am gentle and humble in heart, and you will find rest for your souls. For My yoke is easy and My burden is light" (Matthew 11:28-30).

Evelyn's Potato Salad

10 medium russet potatoes
¼ cup Parmesan cheese, grated
8 boiled eggs, chopped
1 medium carrot, grated
4 medium radishes, grated
½ small onion, chopped

3 T. green olives, sliced with pimentos
1 8-oz. jar sweet pickles, cubed
½ head of cauliflower, cut into
  small pieces
2 tsp. celery seeds
2 cups mayonnaise

Place unpeeled potatoes in a large kettle and cover with water. Bring to boil, reduce heat, and boil gently until potatoes are tender, 15 to 20 minutes.

Drain the water, let the potatoes cool, and then peel and cube them.

Place the potatoes in a large bowl and sprinkle with Parmesan cheese. Gently stir. Add all other ingredients except for the mayonnaise and mix gently.

Place mayonnaise in a medium bowl. Beat with a spoon to make it easier to stir into the salad. Add the mayo to the potato mixture a little bit at a time until you get the consistency and taste you desire.

Serve immediately or refrigerate overnight.

SOUL FOOD
*Better is a dish of vegetables where love is than a fattened ox
served with hatred* (Provers 15:17).

Becky's Potato Soup

48 oz. chicken broth
6 potatoes, peeled and cubed
½ tsp. Mrs. Dash Original Seasoning
1 stick butter
2 pkgs. frozen chopped onions
  (or 4 cups onions, diced)

½ cup all-purpose flour
1¼ cup instant potatoes
salt to taste
pepper to taste
1 qt. half-and-half

Optional
cheddar cheese, grated
bacon bits

Pour chicken broth into a large pot. Add potatoes and Mrs. Dash Original Seasoning. Cook at a quiet boil for 15 to 20 minutes until potatoes are tender.

In a skillet, melt the butter and sauté the onions, cooking until translucent. (Do not let the onions brown.) Add flour and stir, cooking for 5 minutes to form a roux or white sauce. Add 2 cups of the chicken broth from the pot of potatoes. Stir frequently. If there are lumps, add more liquid and pour into a food processor. Blend until smooth and creamy.

Remove potatoes from the chicken broth and set aside. Bring the broth to a boil, and then remove from heat. Add the instant potatoes and blend thoroughly. Slowly add the half-and-half, stirring constantly. Return the pot to the stove and cook 10 minutes on medium low heat (do not let boil). Add the flour mixture to the pot and stir with a whisk. If you want the soup to be thicker, puree some of the cooked potatoes in a blender and add them to the soup.

Return the cooked potatoes to the creamy mixture in the pot. Add salt and pepper to taste.

Top with grated cheddar cheese or bacon bits and serve.

Tip: The soup will thicken as it stands.

"SERVE WITH" SUGGESTIONS

Sweet, Sweet Potato Casserole

3 cups sweet potatoes, freshly
   cooked or canned, and mashed
1 cup white sugar
1 tsp. vanilla

½ cup melted butter
2 eggs, beaten
nonstick cooking spray

Topping

1 cup light brown sugar
¹/₃ cup all-purpose flour

½ cup chopped pecans
¼ cup butter, not melted

Mix all ingredients together and put in a greased casserole dish.

Mix topping ingredients until crumbly, and sprinkle over sweet potato mixture.

Bake at 350° for 30 minutes.

SOUL FOOD

He causes the grass to grow for the cattle, and vegetation for the labor of man, so that he may bring forth food from the earth (Psalm 104:14).

"SERVE WITH" SUGGESTIONS

FRUIT SALADS

Fruit Chipotle Chutney

4 cups of fruit, fresh or frozen
2 T. chipotle peppers in adobo sauce, finely chopped (the more peppers, the spicier the chutney)
1 cup apple, finely chopped
½ cup white vinegar

⅓ cup honey
⅓ cup white sugar
3 T. mustard seeds
½ tsp. salt
½ tsp. ground ginger

Mix all ingredients in a pan. Cook, uncovered on top of the stove at medium heat for approximately 25 minutes or until thickened.

Remove from stove and allow to cool.

Store in an airtight container and place in the refrigerator.

Optional: Place in a food processor and puree for a few seconds until slightly smooth.

Creamy Fruit Salad

¾ cup sugar
1 8-oz. pkg. cream cheese
1 12-oz. pkg. frozen strawberries
1 8-oz. tub Cool Whip

1 10-oz. can crushed pineapple drained
2 large bananas, sliced into rounds
1 cup mini marshmallows

Optional: ½ cup nuts

Whip sugar and cream cheese together. Add remaining ingredients. Chill and serve.

SOUL FOOD

The fruit of the spirit is love, joy, peace, patience, kindness, goodness, faithfulness, gentleness, self-control; against such things there is no law (Galatians 5:22-23).

"SERVE WITH" SUGGESTIONS

Fresh Fruit Salad

2 cups apples, cored, sliced or diced, with or without peel

1 cup bananas, not too ripe, cut into round slices

1 cup grapes, white, red, or both

1 cup peaches, fresh or canned, diced

1 cup oranges or mandarin oranges, canned, cut into pieces

1 cup strawberries, fresh or frozen, cut into pieces

½ cup coconut, toasted and shredded

Drain canned fruit, and then mix all fruit in a large bowl.

Just before serving, sprinkle toasted, shredded coconut on top.

Tip: Any fruit you enjoy will be great in this salad, so be creative.

BREADS

Mom's Biscuits

submitted by Alice Click

MY HUSBAND, KARL, THINKS IT'S FUNNY when I explain how to make Mom's special biscuits that we call "Sylvie Biscuits." It's hard to give a recipe for something I just do, but here it is.

Mix the flour, butter, and milk together. Now, you have to put enough milk in there, but not too much. Work the dough, but not too long.

I use canola oil and bake the biscuits in a square, glass baking dish. I think this really makes a difference in how they turn out. Preheat the glass dish. This is the key to getting the biscuits to rise quickly. Because Mom would preheat her biscuit pan with a scoop of Crisco melting in it, that's what I do.

She would take the biscuit dough that had been cut into large, round shapes (if you don't have a biscuit cutter you can use the top of a glass dipped in flour) and flop each biscuit individually into the hot grease. Then she placed it in the hot oven. This caused the biscuit to have a brown, crunchy bottom. Mom loved to take the bottom of the biscuit and dip it into her coffee. I can see her doing it as I write this. She always made everything look so yummy. I bake them just like I would a cake: 350 degrees—at least in my oven. Yours may need to be 400 degrees.

If you'd like more conventional instructions…

"SERVE WITH" SUGGESTIONS

Sylvie Biscuits

2 cups self-rising flour
⅓ cup butter
¾ cup milk or buttermilk

Additional flour for rolling out the
  biscuits
Crisco shortening or nonstick
  cooking spray

Place the self-rising flour in a large bowl. Cut in the butter until the mixture resembles coarse crumbs. Stir in milk until the flour mixture is moistened.

Turn the biscuit dough onto a lightly floured surface. Using additional flour to keep the dough from sticking to the surface, roll the dough to a ½-inch thickness. Cut out the desired biscuit size and place on a lightly greased cookie sheet.

Bake at 400° for 8 to 10 minutes or until golden brown.

Serve warm!

SOUL FOOD

*This is the bread which comes down out of heaven,
so that one may eat of it and not die*
(John 6:50).

Cornbread

1 8.5-oz. pkg. Jiffy corn muffin mix
3 eggs
¼ cup vegetable oil

½ cup sour cream
¼ cup sugar

Ignore package instructions. Instead, stir muffin mix, eggs, oil, sour cream, and sugar together. Pour into a greased pan.

Bake at 350° for 20 minutes or until a toothpick inserted in the center pulls out cleanly.

Hush Puppies...
Required with Catfish!

by Annie Chapman

L EGEND HAS IT THAT "HUSH PUPPIES" originated in the Civil War days. Southerners would sit around the campfire preparing their supper. If they'd heard that Yankees were near, they would toss their dogs some of the fried cakes and command "Hush, puppies!" to keep them quiet. I don't know if that's true, but it sure makes a lot of sense...and it's a fun story.

Our family has always enjoyed the tasty round bites. And we're especially fond of the ones we used to get when we lived close to a "greasy spoon" that specialized in fried catfish, hush puppies, and cole slaw. I'm not sure how our arteries survived (perhaps we had youth on our side), but we loved to go to Captain Paulo's Catfish Diner and eat our fill.

The following recipe, Chapman's Chin-lickin'-good Hush Puppies, isn't the original from Captain Paulo's, but after many attempts my family agrees it's close enough to be delicious and a family favorite.

Chapman's Chin-lickin'-good Hush Puppies

cooking oil, 2 inches in skillet
2 cups finely ground white cornmeal
   (if you use self-rising cornmeal,
   omit baking soda and salt)
1 T. sugar
2 tsp. baking soda

2 tsp. salt
1 T. yellow onion, minced
1 egg
1 cup buttermilk
4½ T. cold water

Optional
jalapenos or mild chilies, chopped

Heat cooking oil to 365° in a deep fat fryer or deep, heavy pot.

Put the cornmeal in a large mixing bowl.

In a small bowl, mix the sugar, baking soda, salt, and onion. Add the egg and buttermilk, and beat until foamy. Pour all at once into the cornmeal and stir lightly to mix. Add just enough cold water to make the dough the right consistency for dropping into oil. (The dough should be thick enough to drop from the spoon slowly but easily.)

Using a tablespoon, drop one ball at a time into the hot oil. Fry each one for 2 to 3 minutes or until golden brown. Keep turning the "puppies" until all sides are evenly brown.

Remove from oil and place on paper towels to drain. Place hush puppies, uncovered, in warm oven until they're all cooked and you're ready to serve.

Tip: You won't want to serve this every day, but why not treat your family to this special treat every once in a while? Be sure to take a nice long walk as a family as soon as everyone can pry themselves off the couch.

Mama's Best Hush Puppies

3 cups peanut oil	1 medium onion, finely chopped
1 cup self-rising cornmeal	3 T. jalapeno peppers, seeds
½ cup Bisquick	removed, finely chopped
¼ cup Italian bread crumbs	1 tsp. kosher salt
2 eggs	1 tsp. ground black pepper
ice-cold water	

In a deep fat fryer or deep, heavy pot heat peanut oil to 350°.

Mix cornmeal, Bisquick, bread crumbs, and eggs in a small bowl. Slowly stir in small amounts of cold water until the dough is thick and moist. Add onions, chopped peppers, salt, and pepper.

Drop tablespoon dollops into hot oil and deep fry until golden brown.

SOUL FOOD
You know the grace of our Lord Jesus Christ, that though He was rich, yet for your sake He became poor, so that you through His poverty might become rich (2 Corinthians 8:9).

"SERVE WITH" SUGGESTIONS

Zucchini Bread

This is a great way to get your kids to eat a vegetable they might otherwise refuse to try. By the end of the summer, with my garden overrun by zucchini, I look for all kinds of ways to use this squash.

nonstick cooking spray
3 cups self-rising flour (or 3 cups
    all-purpose flour, ¼ tsp. baking
    powder, and 1 tsp. salt)
1 tsp. baking soda
3 T. cinnamon
3 eggs

3 T. vanilla
2¼ cups sugar
1 cup oil
3 cups zucchini, grated (include
    skin and juice)
1 cup walnuts (or pecans), chopped

Lightly grease 3 medium-sized loaf pans.

Sift flour, baking soda, and cinnamon into a large bowl. Add other ingredients and mix well.

Bake at 350° for 1 hour.

Banana Bread

½ cup honey
½ cup vegetable oil
2 eggs, beaten
3 bananas, ripe, mashed
2 cups self-rising flour

1 tsp. baking soda
3 T. milk
½ tsp. vanilla
½ cup chopped walnuts or pecans

Beat honey and oil together. Add eggs and bananas and beat well. Add flour, baking soda, milk, and vanilla. Mix thoroughly. Add nuts and stir.

Bake in a loaf pan or muffin tins at 350° approximately 1 hour or until solid and brown.

Fresh Peach Muffins

nonstick cooking spray or paper
  muffin cups
1 egg
1 cup milk
¼ cup shortening, melted,
  or cooking oil
⅔ cup sugar

¼ tsp. vanilla
½ tsp. salt
¼ tsp. cinnamon
1 tsp. lemon juice
2 cups all-purpose flour
1 cup (overflowing) of fresh peaches,
  unpeeled and chopped

Grease muffin tins or have paper baking cups ready in muffin tins.

Beat the egg, and then stir in milk, shortening, sugar, vanilla, salt, cinnamon, and lemon juice.

Sift together the flour and baking powder, and then stir into milk mixture until just blended. Don't over mix.

Fold in peaches.

Pour into muffin cups, approximately ⅔ full.

Bake at 350° until lightly brown and firm.

SOUL FOOD

When you pass through the waters, I will be with you; and through the rivers, they will not overflow you. When you walk through the fire, you will not be scorched, nor will the flame burn you (Isaiah 43:2).

"SERVE WITH" SUGGESTIONS

Part 6
DESSERTS

Desserts

No meal is quite complete
without the taste of something sweet!

This little poem may be short in words, but it's long on truth. Hardly anything puts an exclamation point on a great meal of wild game than a tantalizing treat. But I'm reminded of a remark Annie's mother, Sylvia, the youngest of her Grandma Naomi's six children, made one day. Her words remind us of what it means to truly love others. She said,

> I grew up thinking my mom didn't like apple pie because so many times I saw her give her slice to others to eat, especially our visitors. I didn't realize until I was older that what gave her more pleasure than the sweetness of the pie was the smile on someone else's face when they were enjoying it.

DESSERTS

PIES & COBBLERS

Annie's Apple Pie

Pie shells

2 cups all-purpose flour, sifted	6 T. Crisco shortening
1 tsp. salt	6 T. milk
4 T. butter	

Pie Filling

1 cup sugar	6 to 8 apples, pared, cored,
2 T. all-purpose flour	and thinly sliced or grated
1 tsp. ground cinnamon	(approximately 6 cups)
½ tsp. ground nutmeg	2 T. butter
dash of salt	

Pie Shells

In a medium bowl, sift the flour and salt together. Cut in shortening and butter with a pastry blender. Add milk and gently stir with fork until well mixed. (Add more flour if needed for best consistency.)

Divide in half to form two balls. Sprinkle flour on counter or bread board. Place each dough ball on the counter, and roll out to form round circles slightly larger than the pie plate.

Place one circle on the pie plate and gently conform the dough to the plate. The other one will go on top of pie filling.

Pie Filling

In a large bowl, combine sugar, flour, spices, and salt. Add sliced apples and mix until apples are well covered.

Place the apple mixture in the pie pan over the pastry shell. Dot apples with butter.

Add the top pie shell, and cut slits so the steam can escape. Crimp the pie shells edges together to seal the edges. Sprinkle top with sugar.

Bake at 400° for 50 minutes or until pie crust is a golden brown.

Old-fashioned Custard Pie

1 cup sugar
4 T. flour
1 cup boiling water
1 egg

1 tsp. lemon extract
3 T. cider vinegar
1 pie shell, baked

In a pan, mix sugar and flour together. Add boiling water, stir, and cook for 5 minutes on medium heat.

Beat the egg and add to the sugar mixture. Cook for 2 minutes, and then add the lemon and vinegar. Cook, stirring constantly, until a smooth, pudding consistency.

Pour the mixture into the pie shell. Let cool and serve. Refrigerate leftovers—if there are any!

DESSERTS

A Simply Delicious Pleasure

IN ADDITION TO ANNIE'S DELIGHTFUL DESSERTS that will satisfy our sweet tooth, we want to include a recipe that I (Steve) enjoy—and willingly drive several hours from home to consume.

For the past few years I've been privileged to hunt in Indiana with my friend Don Hicks. I deeply value the "therapy" of our fellowship and the chasing critters we do in his part of the world. But there's another reason I show up at his door. I know that when I arrive, more than likely there'll be a fresh batch of his wife's fried pies waiting for me on the kitchen counter. Doris has mastered the creation of this delectable treat. And let me tell you, there's absolutely nothing like pouring a hot cup of herb tea sweetened with honey from a Thermos and unwrapping one or two of Doris's fried pies while sitting in a deer stand on a cold November morning. The combination makes me really glad I'm alive...and visiting Indiana!

Doris has graciously agreed to share her recipe with our family and yours.

Doris's Lip-smackin' Fried Pies

1 can Pillsbury Grands biscuits (or similar)	16 oz. applesauce or apple butter* 2 T. butter and ½ cup cooking oil

In a large skillet, heat oil and butter on medium-high.

Open biscuits and roll each one out to about ¼-inch thick.

Put ¼ cup apple filling on one half of a biscuit, fold it over to make a pie, and press the edges together with a fork to seal.

Slide biscuits into the skillet and cook until golden brown. Turn them and brown other side. Remove and drain on layers of paper towels.

Repeat until all pies are done.

* If you don't have homemade apple butter, spice up the applesauce by adding 1 tsp. cinnamon, ½ tsp. nutmeg, and ¼ tsp. cloves. Feel free to add more of these spices until you get the taste you desire.

Perfect Peach Cobbler

1 16-oz. can sliced peaches, drained
1 cup milk
1 cup sugar
1 cup self-rising flour
1 stick butter, melted

In a large bowl combine all ingredients except the butter. Mix slightly (it's okay if there are lumps).

Melt the butter in a loaf pan or square baking dish.

Pour the peach concoction into the melted butter.

Bake at 350° for 50 minutes or until done. The edges should be a deep, golden brown. Make sure the crust in the middle is done.

CAKES

Quick and Easy Cheesecake

2 8-oz. pkgs. cream cheese
2/3 cup sugar
8 oz. sour cream
2 tsp. vanilla

16 oz. Cool Whip
2 graham cracker pie crusts, already
  prepared
1 12-oz. can cherry pie filling

In a large bowl, mix cream cheese, sugar, sour cream, and vanilla. Beat until smooth with an electric mixer.

Gently fold in the Cool Whip.

Pour into the pie crust pans and chill in the refrigerator for one hour.

Remove from refrigerator, top with pie filling, and serve.

SOUL FOOD
*I would feed you with the finest of the wheat, and with
honey from the rock I would satisfy you*
(Psalm 81:16).

DESSERTS

Easter's Delicious Apple Cake

STEVE'S LATE GRANDMOTHER, EASTER DAISY CHAPMAN, wife of the late George Stonewall Chapman and mother of 11 children, was known throughout Logan County, West Virginia, for her wonderful apple cake. Unfortunately, as far as we know, her recipe was never written down. But that doesn't stop the entire Chapman Clan from doing their best to duplicate the unbelievably delicious cake.

Every time I bake anything connected with apples and sugar, my mind goes back to that cake. I've come to believe the elusive ingredient that no one can figure out was probably the generous scoop of love that only Easter could offer.

Here's an apple cake recipe that I respectfully call "'It's Almost Easter's Apple Cake."

It's Almost Easter's Apple Cake

1½ cups sugar	1 tsp. vanilla
1 cup vegetable oil	¼ tsp. nutmeg
2 eggs	1 tsp. cinnamon or apple pie spices
2 cups all-purpose flour	½ tsp. salt
1 tsp. baking soda	3 cups tart apples, thinly sliced

Optional
whipped cream

Grease a 9x13 baking pan.

Mix sugar, oil, and eggs until blended. Beat 1 minute. Stir in remaining ingredients except apples. Beat 1 minute. Stir in apples.

Bake at 350° for 35 to 45 minutes or until wooden toothpick inserted comes out clean.

Tip: This cake doesn't need icing, but it tastes great with a generous dollop of whipped cream.

DESSERTS

CANDIES

Milk and Honey Balls

1¼ cups honey   3 cups powdered skim milk, dry
1½ cups peanut butter

Mix honey and peanut butter. Gradually add dry milk, mixing well.

With greased hands, form dough into small balls. Roll the balls in additional milk powder.

Chill until firm and serve.

Grandma's Molasses Candy

2 cups molasses   pinch of baking soda
1 cup sugar   3 cups black walnuts, chopped
1 T. vinegar   nonstick cooking spray

In a pan, combine molasses, sugar, and vinegar. Cook on low heat until crunchy or brittle when a little is dropped into cold water. The candy thermometer should reach 260°.

Stir in baking soda and nuts.

Pour into greased pan and let set, approximately 5 minutes or until cool.

Break into pieces when cold and serve.

SOUL FOOD

Have I not commanded you? Be strong and courageous!
Do not tremble or be dismayed, for the LORD your God is
with you wherever you go (Joshua 1:9).

DESSERTS

Heavenly Kisses

2 egg whites   ½ tsp. vanilla
½ cup fine, granulated sugar

Beat egg whites until stiff and dry. Beat in 6 tablespoons of sugar, a spoonful at a time, and then beat until peaks form.

Add vanilla and then fold in the rest of the sugar.

Spoon onto cookie sheet and form into "kiss" shape.

Bake at 250° for 50 minutes.

SOUL FOOD
The wise in heart will be called understanding, and sweetness of speech increases persuasiveness (Proverbs 16:21).

DESSERTS

SOUL FOOD

*Since the creation of the world [God's] invisible attributes,
His eternal power and divine nature, have been clearly seen,
being understood through what has been made, so that they
are without excuse* (Romans 1:20).

DESSERTS

Part 7
GRAVIES, MARINADES, AND SAUCES

GRAVIES

Poor Man's Gravy

3 T. bacon drippings, grease, shortening, lard (or 3 T. oil)	1 cup milk or water
¼ cup plus 1 T. all-purpose flour	½ tsp. salt
	½ tsp. pepper

In an iron skillet heat the bacon drippings to hot, but not burning. Stirring as you go, pour small amounts of flour into the grease and cook until the flour turns a nice brown. (Remember, it's easier to add more than to take away.)

Slowly pour milk into the flour mixture. Add as much liquid as you need to achieve the desired consistency of gravy. Add salt and pepper to taste and serve hot.

Tip: Sylvie Biscuits (page 222) taste delicious with this gravy. Let this gravy and biscuit combination remind you of the principles of simplicity…where we work hard and are grateful for what we have. Consider the difference between "making a killing" and "making a living," and remember that a good day is going to sleep with a full belly and a clear conscience.

Tomato Gravy

1 qt. canned, whole tomatoes	2 cups milk
2 T. all-purpose flour	2 T. butter
½ tsp. salt	2 T. sugar
½ cup cream	

Place the tomatoes, including juice, in a saucepan and bring to a boil.

In a separate bowl, blend the flour and salt with the cream. Add the milk and stir.

Pour mixture into the boiling tomatoes, stirring constantly until mixture is thick.

Remove from heat. Stir in butter and sugar. Pour over hot biscuits and serve.

Tip: Sylvie Biscuits (page 222) are great with this recipe.

GRAVIES, MARINADES, AND SAUCES

BRINING SOLUTION

Lindsey's Brining Solution

½ cup kosher salt
¼ cup sugar
thyme

rosemary
crushed juniper berries

To a large bowl of water add salt and sugar. You may also add any fresh (not dried) herbs, such as thyme and rosemary. Crushed juniper berries are a good addition too. Put the meat into the brine and let it sit in the refrigerator for 2 to 3 hours for smaller cuts of meat.

GRAVIES,
MARINADES,
AND SAUCES

MARINADES

Annie's Favorite Marinade

1 T. Worcestershire sauce	1 tsp. cayenne pepper
1 tsp. cumin	2 tsp. apple cider vinegar
1 tsp. paprika	salt and pepper to taste

Mix everything together. If you need to, use a little more Worcestershire sauce so all the other ingredients blend well. The marinade needs to be thick enough to stay on the meat.

Lemon Marinade

1 lemon	
1/3 cup golden raisins	1 tsp. salt
3 T. lemon juice, fresh	½ cup olive oil
1½ tsp. balsamic vinegar	2 T. capers drained

Carefully peel lemon, being careful to avoid the white part of the rind, which is extremely bitter. Cut peel into ½-inch strips and set aside.

Soak raisins in boiling water for 5 minutes. Drain and set aside.

In a small bowl, whisk lemon juice, balsamic vinegar, and salt together. Gradually pour olive oil into mixture, whisking to emulsify (thicken). Stir in lemon zest strips, raisins, and capers.

Multi-meat Marinade

Tip: This marinade is useful for all kinds of game meats as well as beef.

¼ cup cooking oil	1 T. cloves, whole
1 cup onion, chopped	1 T. basil, chopped
1 cup celery, chopped	1 T. thyme
1 cup carrot, chopped	3 bay leaves
8 cups vinegar	½ cup parsley, chopped
4 cups water	1 T. peppercorns, crushed
1 T. allspice berries	6 garlic cloves, crushed

Pour oil in a skillet and sauté the onions, celery, and carrots. Add the rest of the ingredients and simmer for 1 hour. Strain and cool.

Lindsey's Marinade

¼ cup soy sauce	2 T. red wine vinegar
¼ cup olive oil	2 T. minced garlic
2 T. ketchup	1 T. freshly ground black pepper

Mix all ingredients and pour over red meat in a freezer bag. Let meat marinate for 6 to 8 hours, turning every now and then to make sure all of meat gets covered.

Mama's Merry Marinade

Tip: This marinade is great on any red meat.

½ cup peanut oil	$^1/_3$ cup lemon juice
¾ cup soy sauce	½ cup vinegar
¼ cup Worcestershire sauce	5 garlic cloves, pressed and minced
2 T. dry mustard	

Mix together all ingredients and use on your favorite red meat.

Papa's Perfect Wild Game Marinade

Tip: This makes approximately 2 cups of marinade that is really great to use on meat and vegetables.

¼ cup lime juice, fresh	2 cloves garlic, finely chopped
½ cup beef broth	½ tsp. salt
2 tsp. ground cumin	½ tsp. pepper
4 tsp. ground coriander	1¼ cup olive oil

Mix all the ingredients except the oil in a blender. With the blender on low, slowly pour the oil in until everything is mixed well.

Cover and refrigerate until ready to use.

My Deer's Bigger Than Yours Marinade

Tip: This marinade is perfect for red meat or game birds.

½ cup cider or red wine vinegar	2 T. kosher salt
2 garlic cloves, minced	cold water

In a large bowl, mix together all ingredients. Add the frozen or fresh meat and enough water to cover the meat. Soak overnight in the refrigerator.

Venison Marinade

This marinade can be used for any cut of venison except ground. Try this on the best of all venison cuts—backstrap tenderloin.

¾ cup teriyaki sauce	3 cloves garlic, minced
2 T. red wine	¼ tsp. black pepper

Rinse the venison in cold water and pat dry.

In a plastic ziplock bag combine the desired amounts of teriyaki sauce, red wine, garlic, black pepper. Don't add any extra salt since the teriyaki is salty already.

Whatever smells good to you will taste good. Let your nose be your guide.

Marinate the meat for 2 to 24 hours, depending on time available and size of cut (the bigger the cut, the longer the marinating time).

GRAVIES, MARINADES, AND SAUCES

SPICE RUBS

Lindsey's Spice Rub

⅓ cup paprika	2 tsp. dry mustard
¼ cup sugar	2 tsp. cayenne pepper
3 T. black pepper	1 tsp. white pepper
2 T. salt	

Mix all ingredients well and apply to meat.

Dee Dee's Dry Rub

Tip: This marinade is great on any kind of wild game meat.

¼ cup garlic powder	4 T. paprika
3 T. black pepper	2 T. chili powder
1 T. ground cumin	3 T. kosher salt
1 T. onion powder	¼ cup brown sugar

Mix all ingredients together. Keep in a plastic storage bag.

When ready to use, rub directly on the meat and allow to marinate for 2 to 3 hours in the refrigerator before cooking.

GRAVIES, MARINADES, AND SAUCES

BARBECUE AND SWEET & SOUR SAUCES

Betty's Better Barbecue Sauce

1 cup ketchup
4 T. mustard
4 T. vinegar
4 T. sugar

4 T. Worcestershire sauce
1 tsp. kosher salt
dash of hot sauce

Mix all ingredients together in a small pan and simmer for 15 minutes.

Cover and refrigerate overnight.

Pour over meat and simmer for one hour.

Homemade Barbecue Sauce

3 T. butter, melted
1 medium onion, finely chopped
2 stalks celery, finely chopped
½ cup brown sugar
1 tsp. kosher salt
1 T. garlic powder
1 tsp. paprika
1 tsp. hot pepper sauce

1 tsp. dry mustard
2 cups ketchup
2 cups ginger ale
3 T. Worcestershire sauce
3 T. apple cider vinegar
¼ tsp. thyme
¼ tsp. marjoram

Mix all ingredients in a saucepan and simmer for one hour.

Cool and store in the refrigerator.

Lindsey's Sweet and Sour Dressing

1 cup vegetable oil
1 cup sugar
½ cup wine vinegar

3 tsp. soy sauce
dash of salt
pepper to taste

Blend all ingredients well.

247

Sweet and Sour Sauce

1 cup sugar	2 T. cornstarch + 1 tsp. water
½ cup water	2 T. ketchup
½ cup white vinegar	2 tsp. mustard

Combine the sugar, water, and vinegar in a saucepan. Cook until sugar is dissolved, about 5 minutes.

Mix cornstarch with 1 teaspoon of water. Add this to the hot sugar mixture and stir constantly until thickened. Remove from heat.

Let cool for 1 minute and add remaining ingredients.

Sweet and Sour Sauce for Venison and Other Meats

3 cups soup stock or water (if using water, add 2 T. sugar)	1 tsp. pepper
	1 tsp. salt
½ cup ketchup	2 T. sugar
¼ cup ginger, shredded	2 T. vinegar

Put soup stock in a pot and heat to medium high. Add all other ingredients and bring to boil. Then put heat on low and simmer for 10 minutes.

Traditional Sweet and Sour Sauce

Tip: This sauce can be used hot or cold.

⅓ cup rice vinegar	1 tsp. soy sauce
4 T. light brown sugar	2 tsp. cornstarch + 4 tsp. water
1 T. ketchup	

Mix the cornstarch with water until there are no lumps.

Combine all the ingredients in a small saucepan. Bring to a boil, stirring constantly. Let mixture bubble for 1 minute, making sure the sauce looks clear.

GRAVIES, MARINADES, AND SAUCES

DIPPING SAUCES

Homemade Dipping Sauce

½ cup mayonnaise
2 tsp. ketchup
2 T. grated horseradish
$^1/_8$ tsp. oregano

¼ tsp. kosher salt
¼ tsp. paprika
black pepper to taste
$^1/_8$ tsp. cayenne pepper

Mix all ingredients in a bowl. Cool, cover, and store in the refrigerator.

Sweet, Red Onion Marmalade

2 cups red onions or sweet onions,
   sliced
½ cup red wine
2 T. butter

½ cup red wine vinegar
½ cup sugar
salt to taste

Combine all ingredients in a medium saucepan and stir well.

Simmer for 30 minutes over medium heat or until all liquid is cooked off and the onions are translucent.

Homemade Cocktail Sauce

1 cup ketchup
1 T. horseradish, fresh, grated

1 T. lemon juice
1 tsp. Worcestershire sauce

Mix all ingredients in a bowl. Cover and store in the refrigerator.

SOUL FOOD

He who trusts in his riches will fall, but the righteous will flourish like the green leaf. He who troubles his own house will inherit wind, and the foolish will be servant to the wisehearted (Proverbs 11:28-29).

GRAVIES,
MARINADES,
AND SAUCES

Homemade Tartar Sauce

1 cup mayonnaise
¼ cup onion, finely diced
¹/₃ cup sweet pickle relish
¼ tsp. garlic powder

½ tsp. sugar
¼ tsp. marjoram
½ cup brown sugar

Mix all ingredients in a bowl. Cover and store in the refrigerator.

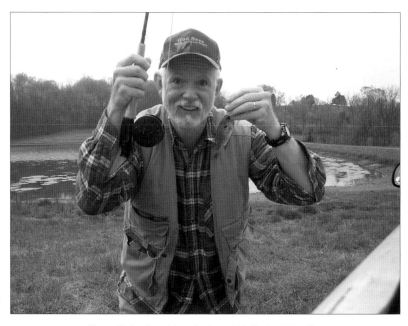

Steve with the fly rod from Annie and his fly-sized bluegill

Part 8
GRILLING

Banned from the Backyard Grill

IT WAS 1977 ON A SUMMER AFTERNOON at our home in Nashville when my Uncle Dan Chapman and his family arrived for a visit. His children were preteens, and when I asked if they were hungry they responded with an excited, belly-growling "Yes!"

Hearing the ravenous tone in our young guests' voices, Annie responded by doing something I've never gotten over. She handed me a bag of charcoal, a can of lighter fluid, a box of matches, and said, "Would you get the fire started and grill the hamburgers for us?"

"Sure thing, babe!" I answered as if I were a grill master. But the truth was, the only grilling I'd ever done was with my dad's old 1963 Biscayne Chevy when I accidentally "grilled" a dog on the highway on my way home from a high school football game. As for cooking freshly ground meat, I was a total novice. Still, I decided to give it a whirl.

I'd watched Annie build a little stack of briquettes on the grate of our little grill before, and I knew enough to douse them with lighter fluid, let the pile soak for a few minutes, and then put a flame to it. That part I managed quite well. However, when Annie brought the plate of nicely formed, uncooked burgers to me, she made the terrible mistake of assuming I had the know-how needed to use that flame to turn raw meat into something humans could consume. She should have known better.

I'll spare you all the pitiful details of what happened in the next several minutes, but here are a few ways I managed to do some serious burger bungling. I "wallered" those burgers all over the backyard. I tossed them on the grill and broke them. I lost sections of meat between the wires of the grate. I even dropped a couple on the grass. Not to be defeated or admit defeat, I quickly picked them up, wiped the grass clippings off, and put them back on the grill. Then, to top everything off, the dripping grease from the meat caused a flare-up of flame that nearly singed my eyebrows off. I looked like I'd been in a vicious fight with our dinner...and lost.

To make the situation worse, my Uncle Dan and his 12-year-old son stood by and watched me as I battled the beef, the grill, and everything else. They silently observed the fiasco. I appreciated them holding back on the comments so I could concentrate on the task at hand.

GRILLING

I finally got all the burgers back on the grill and pieced together. Though several were severely mangled and some contained flecks of grass and sand, at least they started to look done. I was just about ready to transfer them to a plate to deliver to Annie when Dan's boy couldn't hold back his fear any longer.

"Dad?" I could tell a question was about to follow by the way the boy talked and looked pleadingly at his dad.

"Yes, son?"

The youngster pointed at the meaty mess on the grill and said nervously, "Dad, are we gonna have to eat *that*?"

Right then and there I decided to never ever be in charge of grilling again. And that self-imposed ban is still in place today. I have not grilled since 1977! All the guests Annie and I have hosted at backyard barbecues since then will never know how thankful they should be that I put such a policy in place.

Fortunately, when we want the taste of burgers cooked over an open flame and laced with the sweet smell of barbecue, Annie, Nathan, or our son-in-law Emmitt capably take charge. But even the three of them agreed that if this cookbook was going to contain helpful tips on how to manage a grill, there was only one real expert to go to. That person is my hunting buddy Lindsey Williams.

Lindsey is not only a skilled hunter, but we've tasted enough of his cooking exploits to report that he knows his way around the smoke pit. Because he's an expert at both "killin' and grillin' wild game," we asked him to share some backyard barbecue how-tos.

Grilling Tips

by Lindsey Williams

The Grill

- Choose a sturdy grill with good grill grates and a large enough cooking surface to meet your needs.

- A grill with a cover is best because it gives you more cooking options.

- I prefer a charcoal grill over a gas grill because cooking over coals gives more flavor to the food. There are benefits to using gas, such as easy temperature regulation and less steps in the "man make fire" process.

This is where "Lindsey the Grill Meister" works his meat magic!

The Fire

- Hardwood lump charcoal is best because it gives food a more "natural" wood flavor. Hardwood lump charcoal also burns hotter than briquettes.

- Charcoal briquettes are manufactured with products that help bind the briquettes together. In my opinion, these impart a chemical taste to the food.

GRILLING

- Charcoal briquettes burn cooler than hardwood lump charcoal, but they last a bit longer.

- There are charcoal briquettes that will start by just striking a match to them. This type of charcoal gives the strongest chemical taste to whatever is being cooked. If you prefer the taste of petroleum to the taste of what you're cooking, this is the way to go.

- Propane gas grills are easy to light, and the cooking temps can be easily dialed in. But cooking over gas does not give the food the additional flavor that cooking with charcoal does.

- To start your charcoal, you can use lighter fluid or a charcoal chimney. Lighter fluid can be dangerous and leaves a petroleum flavor on what is being cooked. A charcoal chimney starter uses pieces of newspaper to start the coals, avoiding the lighter fluid flavor.

SOUL FOOD

When they got out on the land, they saw a charcoal fire already laid and fish placed on it, and bread. Jesus said to them, "Bring some of the fish which you have now caught."... Jesus said to them, "Come and have breakfast" (John 21:9-10,12).

Grilling Tools

- Tongs and spatula for turning food

- Grilling grid or basket for fish or chopped vegetables

- Wire grill brush or stainless steel pads for cleaning grill

- Flame-retardant glove for handling hot coals and the grill

- Digital meat thermometer for making sure food is thoroughly cooked

- Spray bottle filled with water for spritzing and controlling flare-ups that blacken food

GRILLING

Grill Prep

- Once you have a good, hot fire going, close the grill lid to let the grates get good and hot.

- Then open the grill and use the wire grill brush to clean the grates.

- Before you put food on the grill, take a paper towel soaked in vegetable oil and brush it across the grill's cooking surface using tongs. This keeps the food from sticking to the grill.

- This is also the best time to arrange your fire into zones for direct and indirect cooking. For cooking directly over the coals, make sure the coals extend one inch beyond the surface the meat is going to cook over. For indirect cooking, make sure you have enough surface with no coals underneath to accommodate what you're grilling.

Grilling: Direct and Indirect

Direct Grilling

- If the food will take less than 30 minutes to barbecue, cook directly over the coals. This includes burgers, steaks, fish, small or boneless pieces of fowl, and sausages.

Indirect Grilling

- Foods that take longer than 30 minutes to cook are best cooked over indirect heat. This works best for large cuts of meat like whole tenderloins, backstraps, and turkey breasts.

How-to Steps for Indirect Grilling

- Bank coals on one or both sides of a drip pan that will be placed on the lower grid.

- Sear meat over coals for a minute per side, and then move it to the center of grill over the drip pan.

- Close the grill to contain the heat and seal in the smoky flavor.

- Add apple juice or other flavored beverages to the drip pan, if desired, to provide moistness and flavor to the meat.

- If you want to add more smoke flavor, get wood chips (hickory, cherry, apple, mesquite, oak) and soak them in saltwater for at least 30 minutes. Then wrap the soaked wood chips in foil, punch holes in the top of the foil pouch, and place directly on top of the coals. Make sure you close the top of the grill when cooking to keep that good smoke flavor where the meat is.

Grill Meat Preparation

- Wild game meat can be brined, marinated, or have a spice rub applied, depending on the kind of meat and what you want it to taste like.

- *Brining* makes cooked meat retain moisture. The salt in the brine solution causes the cells of the meat to absorb water via osmosis. The salt then causes the proteins to coagulate, which traps and holds the water molecules. This prevents the meat being grilled from drying out (as long as it's not overcooked). Brining works best on wild birds and hogs. Here's a simple brine recipe:

    To a large bowl of water add ½ cup kosher salt and ¼ cup sugar. You may also add any fresh (not dried) herbs, such as thyme and rosemary. Crushed juniper berries are a good addition too. Put the meat into the brine and let it sit in the refrigerator for 2 to 3 hours for smaller cuts of meat.

- *Marinating* is soaking meat in a seasoned liquid before cooking to add flavor and tenderize. The liquid, or marinade, is usually acidic and contains ingredients such as vinegar, lemon juice, or wine. A marinade often includes oils, herbs, or other spices to add more flavor. The process may last minutes, as in the case of fish, or hours depending on the type and size of the cuts of meat. Check out the Gravies, Marinades, and Sauces section starting on page 239. Here's a simple marinade for red meat, such as venison, elk, and bison:

    ¼ cup soy sauce, ¼ cup olive oil, 2 T. ketchup, 2 T. red wine vinegar, 2 T. minced garlic, 1 T. freshly ground black pepper. Mix all ingredients and pour over red meat in a freezer bag. Let meat marinate for 6 to 8 hours, turning every now and then to make sure all of meat gets covered.

- *Spice rub* is a mixture of ground spices created to add flavor to meat. Sometimes salt is added for flavor, and sugar is included to cause the rub to caramelize. The simplest rub is just coarsely ground black pepper. The spices are rubbed on the meat before cooking, forming a coating. For the flavors to permeate the meat, the rub needs to be on the meat for several hours before cooking. If you want a crust on

GRILLING

the meat or just have the outer portion of the meat flavored, begin cooking immediately after the meat's been coated. So apply the following rub 12 to 24 hours before cooking or just before meat goes on the grill. The longer the rub is on the meat before cooking, the more the meat will be flavored by the spices. The spices are usually coarsely ground. Here's a simple, all-purpose spice rub:

> $^1/_3$ cup paprika, ¼ cup sugar, 3 T. black pepper, 2 T. salt, 2 tsp. dry mustard, 2 tsp. cayenne, 1 tsp. white pepper. Mix all ingredients well and apply to meat.

Grilling Wild Game

- Allow meat to come to room temperature before cooking.

- Wild game is extremely lean and will cook faster than you think. Use a digital thermometer frequently to check the internal temperature of the meat. Overcooking makes wild game dry and tough—think shoe leather.

- Wild game should be cooked to a temperature 10 to 15 degrees less than domestic meat. For example, domestic turkey is done when the thermometer registers 165° to 175°. Wild turkey is well-done at 160°.

- Always take game off the grill when it's 5 to 10 degrees before fully cooked status (as shown on the thermometer). Allow it to "stand" for at least 5 minutes before serving. During this time the internal temperature of the meat will continue to rise. (Yes, it's still cooking, folks!) Letting it stand helps the meat retain more juices.

Recipe Index
Story Index

Recipe Index

Story Index

More Great Books by
Steve & Annie Chapman

Steve Chapman
10 Things I Want My Son to Know
365 Things Every Hunter Should Know
Another Look at Life from a Deer Stand
The Good Husband's Guide to Balancing Hobbies and Marriage
Great Hunting Stories
Hot Topics for Couples
(with Annie Chapman)
A Hunter Sets His Sights
A Look at Life from a Deer Stand
A Look at Life from a Deer Stand Devotional
A Look at Life from a Deer Stand Gift Edition
A Look at Life from a Deer Stand Study Guide
With God on a Deer Hunt

Annie Chapman
10 Ways to Prepare Your Daughter for Life
Hot Topics for Couples
(with Steve Chapman)
Letting Go of Anger
The Mother-in-Law Dance
Overcoming Negative Emotions
What Every Wife Wants Her Husband to Know
A Woman's Answer to Anger

To read sample chapters, go to www.harvesthousepublishers.com.

These books are available at your local Christian bookstore
or you can order them at
www.SteveandAnnieChapman.com